KICKitUP!

Adding **SPICE** to Your **SCRAPBOOK LAYOUTS**

By Greta Hammond and Angelia Wigginton

MEMORY MAKERS BOOKS

CINCINNATI, OHIO

www.mycraftivity.com

13 12 11 10 09   5 4 3 2 1

Distributed in Canada by Fraser Direct
100 Armstrong Avenue
Georgetown, ON, Canada L7G 5S4
Tel: (905) 877-4411

Distributed in the U.K. and Europe by David & Charles
Brunel House, Newton Abbot, Devon, TQ12 4PU, England
Tel: (+44) 1626 323200, Fax: (+44) 1626 323319
E-mail: postmaster@davidandcharles.co.uk

Distributed in Australia by Capricorn Link
P.O. Box 704, S. Windsor, NSW 2756 Australia
Tel: (02) 4577-3555

Library of Congress Cataloging-in-Publication Data

Hammond, Greta.
  Kick it up! / Greta Hammond and Angelia Wigginton.
     p. cm.
  Includes bibliographical references and index.
  ISBN 978-1-59963-040-3 (pbk. : alk. paper)
  1. Photograph albums. 2. Photographs--Conservation and restoration. 3. Scrapbooks.
I. Wigginton, Angelia. II. Memory Makers Books (Firm) III. Title.
  TR465.H33 2009
  745.593--dc22

                              2009004486

Editor: Kristin Boys
Designer: Steven Peters
Production Coordinator: Matt Wagner
Photographers: Al Parrish, Adam Hand
Stylist: Jan Nickum

www.fwmedia.com

METRIC CONVERSION CHART

to convert	to	multiply by
Inches	Centimeters	2.54
Centimeters	Inches	0.4
Feet	Centimeters	30.5
Centimeters	Feet	0.03
Yards	Meters	0.9
Meters	Yards	1.1
Sq. Inches	Sq. Centimeters	6.45
Sq. Centimeters	Sq. Inches	0.16
Sq. Feet	Sq. Meters	0.09
Sq. Meters	Sq. Feet	10.8
Sq. Yards	Sq. Meters	0.8
Sq. Meters	Sq. Yards	1.2
Pounds	Kilograms	0.45
Kilograms	Pounds	2.2
Ounces	Grams	28.3
Grams	Ounces	0.035

ABOUT the AUTHORS

Greta Hammond's real creative passion began when she discovered scrapbooking about eight years ago after her son was born. The outlet it provided was just what she needed after deciding to stay home with her son. Greta has since shared her love of scrapbooking by teaching at local scrapbook stores and has also had the privilege of doing freelance work with a number of industry manufacturers and magazines. She was thrilled to have been chosen a Memory Makers Master in 2007 and inducted into the Creating Keepsakes Hall of Fame in 2006. Greta has been published in numerous magazines and idea books. When she's not creating, she is spending time with her husband and two children at their home in Northern Indiana.

Angelia Wigginton lives in Belmont, Mississippi, with her husband, Rich, their two daughters, Olivia and Michaela, and a trio of cats. She began scrapbooking 11 years ago, after discovering scrapbooking supplies at a local flea market. Since that time her love for all things related to scrapbooking and papercrafting has only grown deeper. As a computer engineer turned stay-at-home mom, she has devoted many hours to this hobby. She describes her style as "linear, clean and colorful." Angelia, a 2006 Memory Makers Master, loves patterned papers, buttons, brads and rub-ons, and delights in finding just the right color scheme or pattern combo to "set the mood" for her photos and stories.

DEDICATION and ACKNOWLEDGMENTS

I dedicate this book to Rich, Olivia, and Michaela. They add the spice to the "pages of my life" with their love, laughter and warmth. In creating this book, I had the pleasure of working with not only a very talented lady, but a dear friend. That her artwork and writing were top-notch was a given, but I could always count on Greta to come up with an idea when I was stuck, and she seemed to make the process of writing a book easier and more fun. Thank you, Greta, for being a great partner!

—Angelia

I dedicate this book to my family; the spice in my life and the reason I scrapbook at all. Thank you for putting up with all my crazy hours and even crazier moods! Love you allways! And to my dear friend Angelia: This process would not have been near as enjoyable without you. Thank you for your constant encouragement, treasured friendship and willingness to take a chance with me.

—Greta

Thanks go to:

Our editors, Christine and Kristin, for their guidance, encouragement and patience.

Our families, for being the joy in our lives and the inspiration for so many of the pages in this book.

Our team—Christine, Denine, Jennifer, Linda, Marla, and Nic—for sharing with us their talents and ideas for this book. You'll agree that they rocked the before and afters.

Our sponsors, for their generous donations. We believe you can't go wrong with their awesome products!

Our contributors, as shown in the gallery in Chapter 6. When we posted our request for layouts with that "extra something," they delivered! We feel happy and honored to include their artwork in our book.

Introduction 6

Chapter 1: Backgrounds 8

Chapter 2: Photos 22

Chapter 3: Titles 36

Chapter 4: Embellishments 54

Chapter 5: Journaling 72

Chapter 6: Gallery 88

Creative Team 122

Source Guide 124

Index 126

my favorite hat

Our first stop on vacation was Lambert's in Foley, Alabama. You and Michaela wanted some "throwed rolls". You loved the rolls, but this cap really captured your heart! And, you wore it constantly for the remainder of our trip, despite my requests for you to "please take off the hat". Olivia and her hat, June, 2008

this hat

Our first stop on vacation was Lambert's in Foley, Alabama. You and Michaela wanted some "throwed rolls". You loved the rolls, but this cap really captured your heart! And, you wore it constantly for the remainder of our trip, despite my requests for you to "please take off the hat". Olivia and her hat, 06/08

You and Kate were adorable in your costumes! We went downtown after school to trick or treat and by the time we got there the sidewalks were full of superheros, witches, animals and scary creatures.

Oct 2007

trick treat

We joined right in and started to collect the good stuff. By then end, your buckets were full and your legs were tired but a good time was had by all!

happy halloween

celebrate olivia's birthday with a family party complete with cake, ice cream, and gifts. her cousin, aunts, uncles, grandma and Poppa with her, eating cupcakes her grandma gifts that were picked just for her. I cannot believe my baby girl is thirteen!

Happy Birthday 13

party time!

we traditionally celebrate olivia's birthday with a family party complete with cake, ice cream, and gifts. she loves it all - having her cousins, aunts, uncles, grandma, and Poppa with her, eating cupcakes her grandma made, and opening gifts.

🌼 my girl

You and Kate were adorable in your costumes! We went downtown after school to trick or treat and by the time we got there the sidewalks were full of superheros, witches, animals and scary creatures.

We joined right in and started to collect the good stuff. By then end, your buckets were full and your legs were tired but a good time was had by all!

trick or treat

Introduction
Get ready to spice things up!

Have you ever spent time working on a scrapbook page and got to the end, only to grumble, "Something is missing," or "It looks OK …"? Or maybe you just started scrapbooking and are stumped about what you can do to take your pages to the next level. Perhaps you've been scrapbooking awhile and find yourself in a rut; you're looking for some new techniques to break the mold and spice up those pages.

If so, this book is here to help! As scrapbookers, we strive to make our scrapbook pages into pieces of artwork we can be proud of. However, we don't always know how to get them to that place of honor. Most of us could use a little help every now and then. In the pages of this book. we give you visual tools to help take your layouts up a notch. You'll find this book is packed full of before and after illustrations where we take a good page and then kick it up to the next level by making just a few changes. The results are amazing, and the techniques are simple to follow. Plus, there's a gallery jam-packed with examples of kicked-up layouts for loads of inspiration. To make it easy to get started, we target specific areas for improvement: backgrounds, photos, titles, embellishments and journaling. This is your hands-on reference to refer back to whenever you're faced with a "what's missing?" dilemma. So jump in and take a look. Find an example, give it a try and watch your pages go from nice to wow!

aquarium Life

Just a small sampling of our adventures at Mystic Aquarium. I love all the colors and textures within the exhibits. From penguins and sea lions to fish and sting rays, there is so much to see and explore in one afternoon visit.

Original

Just a small sampling of our adventures at Mystic Aquarium. I love all the colors and textures within the exhibits. From penguins and sea lions to fish and sting rays, there is so much to see and explore in one afternoon visit.

aquarium life

Kicked up!

mystic

Chapter 1: Backgrounds

Photographers, cinematographers and art curators all know the importance of arranging attractive and appropriate backgrounds and settings. The right background enhances the theme of a set, highlights a picture's subjects and shows off beautiful paintings effectively. We can apply the same principles to highlight the photographs, journaling and memorabilia we include on our scrapbook pages.

It all starts with the foundation of the page—the background papers and elements. The patterns and colors you choose can accent your photos, or they can distract from the story you want to tell. This chapter includes illustrations for kicking up your background using a variety of techniques and elements like popped-up die-cuts, detailed hand-stitching, distressing and edge treatments and changing pattern and color. You'll find that switching up your backgrounds can take your scrapbook pages to the next level.

Original

This layout showcases a fun set of photos that perfectly illustrate my son's excitement over his new skateboard. He was thrilled with his new possession and couldn't wait to show it off. These grungy-looking background papers in all-boy colors were the perfect complement to the skater-dude photos. The bright orange and red serve to highlight my son's grinning face.

Supplies: Patterned paper, stickers (Little Yellow Bicycle); buttons, chipboard (BasicGrey); Misc: Palatino Linotype font

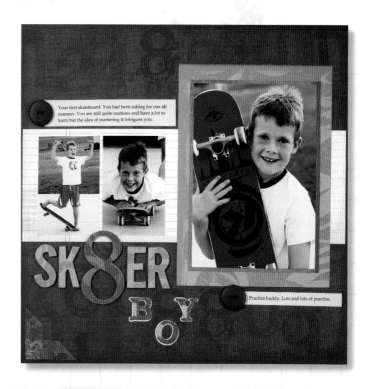

Kicked Up!

Though the background papers in the original layout complement the theme, they're a bit static on their own. On this layout, I added some complementary orange flourishes to opposite corners of the background, which draw the eye toward the center (to the photos) while giving the layout a sense of movement. Just a few quick changes can spice up a layout so well!

Supplies: Patterned paper, stickers (Little Yellow Bicycle); buttons, chipboard (BasicGrey); Misc: Palatino Linotype font

QUICK TIP
Look for interesting designs within your pattern papers, and then cut them out to make unique backgrounds.

Original

My daughter seems to have a bit of a flair for the dramatic, and loves anything that includes pink and sparkles. She reins us all in for her performances complete with costumes and music. These photos of one such moment begged, of course, for a perfectly pink background and some bling. I offset the linear design with a pair of fluttering butterflies adorned with gems.

Supplies: Cardstock; patterned paper, brads, rub-ons (Little Yellow Bicycle); letters (American Crafts); die-cuts (Provo Craft); gems (Westrim); Misc: ink, Tahoma font

Kicked Up!

Although the original layout is cute and pink, the background with its straight lines wasn't quite soft and interesting enough for such a dramatic, girly theme. This layout takes the theme a few steps further with a background of lacy details and pink ribbon. Framing the page in scalloped edges brings it from "pretty" to "pretty fabulous"!

Supplies: Cardstock; patterned paper, brads, rub-ons (Little Yellow Bicycle); chipboard (American Crafts); die-cuts (Provo Craft); gems (Westrim); Misc: ink, punch, Tahoma font

Original

Disney World! There really is nothing quite like it. Our trip was as magical as they proclaim it to be. The kids were speechless for the first few minutes in the gate, not knowing what to expect but yet not expecting it to be this amazing! This page is meant to illustrate that magical feeling through bright photos, vivid colors and fun details. The layout is simple and to the point, but effective nonetheless.

Supplies: Cardstock; patterned paper, chipboard, buttons, rub-ons (Scenic Route); stickers (Scenic Route, Making Memories); transfer foil (Stix2Anything); Misc: Tahoma font

Kicked Up!

While there is nothing technically wrong with the first layout, who could argue that Mickey ears don't make a much better backdrop for a Disney layout? This page is instantly taken up a notch with an extra-large set of those famous ears. The lines are still simple and geometric, but the feeling is so much more powerful. Plus, you know what the page is about before you even read a word.

Supplies: Cardstock; patterned paper, chipboard, buttons, rub-ons (Scenic Route); stickers (Scenic Route, Making Memories); transfer foil (Stix2Anything); Misc: Tahoma font

Original

First birthdays only come once, and Marla has captured her daughter's day with this adorable photo and colorful design. With the evidence right on her face, there's no doubt Adeline was enjoying her cake! Marla used blocks of fun, brightly colored patterned papers across the bottom of her layout to resemble little packages and convey her party theme. The ribbon bow tops off the biggest package of all—the photos—and neatly ties the whole page together.

Supplies: Patterned paper (Scenic Route); die-cut paper (Making Memories); letters, ribbon (American Crafts); Misc: circle punches, Georgia font

Kicked Up!

One quick way to jazz up a layout is to think outside the box when it comes to the shape of the background. Marla put a new twist on the traditional square background by using a bracket shape instead. This layout is nearly identical to the original in design, but its background shape makes it so much more exciting! Plus, curved perimeters that move in and out draw the eye toward the center of the layout where the title and photos lie.

Supplies: Patterned paper (Scenic Route); die-cut paper (Making Memories); letters, ribbon (American Crafts); Misc: circle punches, Georgia font

Original

Sometimes one special photo deserves a layout of its own, and it doesn't take much to create a page that shows it off. Choosing soft colors like tan and blue enhances the seaside theme on this page, with the green glitter letters highlighting the color of the grass. I rested the photo on a simple and subtle blue background print and topped off the design with butterfly accents. The large one balances the size of the photo.

Supplies: Cardstock; patterned paper (BasicGrey, KI Memories); letters (American Crafts); rub-ons (Deja Views, Scenic Route); Misc: Times New Roman font

Kicked Up!

Although I was happy with the overall design of the first page, the background was a little flat for such a fabulous photo. Using a basic circle punch, you can add immediate drama to your background with paper scraps; I did mine in varying shades of blue and green, which give this layout a look similar to the original—but better! The pink butterflies were a bit generic and didn't match the beach theme, so I opted for transparent, more natural-looking critters for this kicked-up page.

Supplies: Cardstock; patterned paper (BasicGrey, Scenic Route, KI Memories, Fancy Pants, Chatterbox, SEI, Me & My Big Ideas, 7Gypsies, Autumn Leaves); chipboard butterfly, rub-ons (Scenic Route); rub-on butterflies (BasicGrey); letters (American Crafts); Misc: circle punch, ink, button, transparency, pen, Times New Roman font

Original

My sister's cat, Meeko, provides lots of entertainment for Michaela, whether he wants to or not. Mixing patterned papers with a page torn from an old book creates a varied, warm look for the background. Lining up the boldest background pattern with the main photo serves to highlight it. Butterflies cut from the pattern make for quick, custom embellishments that coordinate with the page's backdrop.

Supplies: Patterned paper (SEI, BasicGrey, Scenic Route); rub-ons (Deja Views); letters (American Crafts); Misc: book page, Times New Roman font

Kicked Up!

Sometimes a layout needs just a couple small changes in the background design to take it from "good" to "great." You'll first notice the addition of the striped paper and the black lined paper. Both help balance the loud patterned paper and help create a photo frame. Tilting the photos (and frame) is that unexpected detail that takes the page to the next level.

Supplies: Patterned paper (BasicGrey, October Afternoon, Scenic Route); letters (American Crafts); brads (Fancy Pants); Misc: book page, Times New Roman font

Original

I never dreamed a hat could make my oldest daughter so happy, but once she bought this one, she wore it everywhere with this same smile. Keeping the page simple and graphic, I chose a brown background and mixed it with khaki and green patterned papers. Rub-on words combined with alphabet stickers make for an easy, if somewhat uninspired, title.

Supplies: Cardstock; patterned paper (KI Memories, Fontwerks, Scenic Route); rub-ons (Scenic Route); letters (American Crafts); brad (Making Memories); photo turn (7Gypsies); Misc: corner rounder, Times New Roman font

Kicked Up!

On this layout, I amped up the original green strip of background paper to provide a more lively backdrop. I combined my title, embellishment and journaling into an energetic border that really stands out. I mixed up the original green pattern with a lighter print for more pizzazz. The snazzy title and die-cut arrow lead the eye directly to the photos. Finally, the flowers balance and soften the background and provide sweet detail.

Supplies: Cardstock: patterned paper (KI Memories, Fontwerks, Fancy Pants); rub-ons, arrow (Scenic Route); letters (American Crafts); brads, buttons (Making Memories); photo turns (7Gypsies); flowers (Prima); Misc: corner rounder, Times New Roman font

Original

The beluga whale exhibit is always our first stop in the door at Mystic Aquarium. We all seem to get caught up in their huge white bodies and repetitive behavior. Before long, we have stood there for 10 minutes without realizing it. These two photos capture the experience well. Because there is so much blue in the photos, I chose a neutral color scheme to complement them while still allowing them to star on the page.

Supplies: Cardstock; patterned paper (October Afternoon); stickers (Scrapworks, October Afternoon); button (Scenic Route); Misc: Antique Olive font

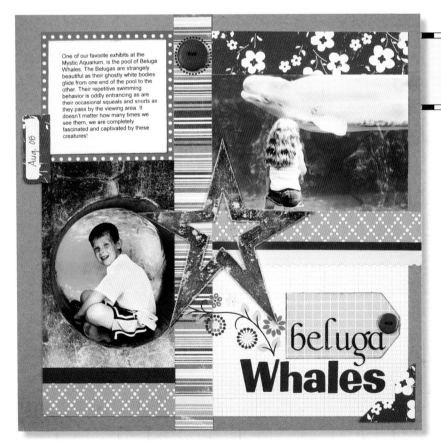

Kicked Up!

While the original layout's neutral-colored background doesn't compete with the photos, it feels a bit dull. The color-blocked background on this kicked-up layout, however, energizes the page without distracting from the photos. The blocks of paper are strategically placed to frame the photos and to attract the eye. In addition, the new page background feels more cohesive by tying all the separate elements together.

Supplies: Cardstock; patterned paper (October Afternoon); star (Scenic Route); stickers (Scrapworks, October Afternoon); transfer foil (Stix2Anything); button (BasicGrey); rub-on (American Crafts); Misc: Antique Olive font

Original

Ice cream three times a day?! Our kids would want to go live with Denine! Denine chose hot, bright colors in simple patterns to accent these shots of her son enjoying his summertime treat. The die-cut sticker border and multi-colored title lend a happy feel to this layout.

Supplies: Cardstock; patterned paper (BasicGrey, Pink Martini); stickers (BasicGrey); chipboard (Scenic Route); brads (Making Memories); buttons (Autumn Leaves, Creative Imaginations); digital brush (Shabby Princess); ribbon (Offray); Misc: floss

Kicked Up!

Wanting to echo more of the crazy energy that her son exhibits when devouring his ice cream, Denine chose four punchier patterns to mix and match for the background. The combination creates a zany style, but the use of similar colors pulls off the look successfully. Our favorite addition to the page is the zigzag edge she added to her photo mats.

Supplies: Cardstock; patterned paper (BasicGrey); photo corners (Fancy Pants); brads (Making Memories, Heidi Swapp, Stemma); buttons (BasicGrey, My Mind's Eye); stickers (BasicGrey, 7Gypsies); letters (American Crafts); ribbon (KI Memories, Offray); Misc: floss

QUICK TIP

You can easily fake stitches on a page. Just poke holes with a threadless needle and connect the dots using a pen.

Original

Olivia doesn't eat a variety of fruits, but she rarely turns down a banana. After an energetic swim in the lake, she was ready for such a snack. These photos show a bit of her silly side (versus that moody, pouty side), so I chose lighthearted, whimsical prints to coordinate with the colors of her swimsuit and the grass. Wide strips of patterned papers serve as a simple background on which to rest the photos.

Supplies: Cardstock (Bazzill); patterned paper (BasicGrey); flowers, brad (Making Memories); rub-on (Scenic Route); Misc: buttons, Times New Roman font

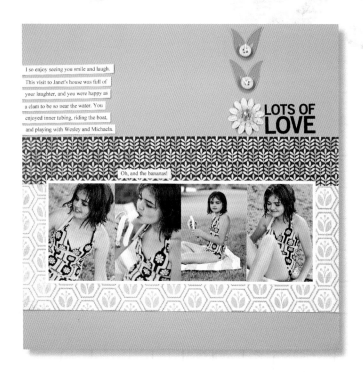

Kicked Up!

To highlight the playful photos, I took my background design up a creative notch on this page, cutting along the geometric lines of the honeycomb print. Using that piece as my guide, I cut similar shapes from my darker floral print and used the hand-cut strips as the background for my photos. I also switched the solid green cardstock to a subtle pattern to give the page some dimension and flair. The layout is similar to the original layout, but the hand-cut background gives it lots of spice!

Supplies: Cardstock; patterned paper, letters (BasicGrey); stickers (BasicGrey, Making Memories); transparency (Hambly); Misc: Times New Roman font

Original

No matter how many times we visit, it seems that the Mystic Aquarium always has something new to offer. This layout is all about the creatures we encountered on our recent visit. The fish tank photo is engaging and colorful, so it serves as the focal point on top of a simple, neutral background. I arranged a strip of smaller photos at the bottom of the page to balance the weight of the larger main photo and to provide more of a visual story of our day.

Supplies: Cardstock; patterned paper, stickers, buttons (BasicGrey); Misc: Letter Gothic font

Kicked Up!

While the original page shows off my photos well, it doesn't do much to grab attention. The straight lines feel generic, and the colors are bland. In comparison, this second layout boasts a much more exciting backdrop. The curve in the patterned paper provides energy and movement like you would anticipate finding in an aquarium. As a result, the eye immediately follows the main photo through the page to the journaling, title and supporting photos and quickly sees the playful mood of the layout.

Supplies: Cardstock; patterned paper, buttons (BasicGrey); letters (Li'l Davis); tab (October Afternoon); rub-ons (Basic Grey, October Afternoon); Misc: Letter Gothic font

Original

As family photographers, we are often faced with the uncooperative subject like my daughter. Taking my color cues from the photos, I chose blues and greens for the background, but in lighter shades than my daughter's shirt so she would stand out. The fun title echoes the "look" in the photos.

Supplies: Cardstock; patterned papers (KI Memories, Scenic Route, October Afternoon); brads (KI Memories); letters (Scenic Route, Mustard Moon); tag (Making Memories); die-cut (K&Co.); Misc: flower, Arial font

Kicked Up!

Although the original layout is balanced, the elements fail to communicate the story—the colors and patterns are sweet, while the photos are more silly. Using bright, bold colors in a background treatment helps tell a spunky story more effectively. I crafted a lively background in bright patterns shaped in hand-cut waves to create energy and match my daughter's attitude. Plus the colors contrast with the photos, which serves to highlight them.

Supplies: Cardstock; patterned papers (Scenic Route, Making Memories); letters (American Crafts); tags, buttons (Making Memories); rub-ons (Scenic Route); Misc: Arial font

A little glimpse into our day in downtown Chicago. Vicki and I saw it all and took pictures of most of it! We started out at the north end of the loop, and made our way to the theatre district where we had seen Wicked the night before. Totally fun just taking in the sights, with a little shopping thrown in for good measure!

Chicago

Original

A little glimpse into our day in downtown Chicago. Vicki and I saw it all and took pictures of most of it! We started out at the north end of the loop and made our way to the theatre district where we had seen Wicked the night before. Totally fun just taking in the sights, with a little shopping thrown in for good measure!

A GLIMPSE OF Chicago

Kicked up!

Chapter 2: Photos

If a picture is worth a thousand words, then our albums sure have a lot to say! Along with the stories, photos are the most significant element of a scrapbook page. They are visual reminders of our memories and often say more than any words can. It's doubtful that many of us would scrap so much if we didn't have all these photos piling up! The convenience of digital photography and the mainstream use of photo-editing programs has provided us with even more pictures, as well as the ability to improve and enhance our photos at the touch of a button. This convenience, which provides lots of options, can also come with confusion and frustration, resulting in lackluster page designs as we resort to the same easy method over and over again. Just because a photo is shaped like a box doesn't mean your ideas have to be square. From adding products like acrylic details and digital frames, to tips for getting a better picture, this chapter shows a variety of options to provide that instant spice to your pages.

Original

The first day of school is an exciting day for my daughters, even though they dread rising early. These waiting-for-the-bus shots have lots of color, so I chose a neutral background and patterned paper in similar colors, using them in small pieces to frame the photos. Label stickers and a sparkly chipboard title complete the look.

Supplies: Cardstock; patterned paper (BasicGrey, Fancy Pants); chipboard (American Crafts); labels (Collage Press); letters (Making Memories); Misc: Arial font

Kicked Up!

While the original layout features my daughters, the photos could tell a better story. The photos are too similar. and although the title mentions the bus, you don't see one on the page. This layout shows how you can boost the impact of your layout by photographing your subjects from different angles and distances. Take more photos than you think you'll need, and then use a variety of shots to tell your story.

Supplies: Cardstock; patterned paper (BasicGrey); letters (KI Memories, Making Memories); labels (Collage Press); Misc: Arial font

Original

I still have a little chuckle when I look at these pictures from our little find this fall. Having fun certainly doesn't have to be fancy or cost a lot! And neither does making a good layout. These earth-tone papers and simple embellishments make the perfect backdrop for the hillbilly slide photos. The journaling is neatly tucked behind the main photo, and the rust orange accents provide some color.

Supplies: Cardstock; patterned paper (BasicGrey, Jillibean Soup, Sassafrass); chipboard, button (BasicGrey); stickers (American Crafts); digital frame by Rhonna Farrer (Two Peas in a Bucket); tag (Avery); rub-on (Deja Views); Misc: Times New Roman font

Kicked Up!

With a zoom lens, it's easy to be a lazy photographer. Just stand in one place and click away. But comparing this focal photo and the one on the original page illustrates a reason to make a change. The focal photo here grabs your attention and makes you feel a part of the action. Just getting down on eye level with my son makes the picture—and the entire layout—so much more engaging.

Supplies: Cardstock; patterned paper (BasicGrey, Jillibean Soup); letters (American Crafts); rub-ons (October Afternoon, BasicGrey); brad (Fancy Pants); button (BasicGrey); digital frame by Rhonna Farrer (Two Peas in a Bucket); tag (Avery); Misc: Times New Roman font

QUICK TIP

Instead of cropping out empty space in your photo, make use of it by digitally adding your journaling before printing the photo.

Original

Watching my kids grow and change is often bittersweet. It is fun to witness their accomplishments, but sad to think they are growing up so fast. This layout documents my feelings about my son growing up and the changes he has gone through lately. The papers match the photos perfectly, and my simple design supports a large title and journaling.

Supplies: Patterned paper, chipboard (Fancy Pants); buttons (BasicGrey); stickers (EK Success, American Crafts); Misc: Letter Gothic font

Kicked Up!

Although the original layout is well balanced with a great color scheme, I quickly noticed that the photos appeared flat against the background. By adding a digital frame in Photoshop before printing, the photos are instantly—and easily!—transformed and really pop off the blue background. It goes to show that just a small change can make a huge impact on a layout.

Supplies: Patterned paper, chipboard (Fancy Pants); buttons (BasicGrey); digital brush by Rhonna Farrer (Two Peas in a Bucket); rub-ons (American Crafts, Scenic Route); stickers (EK Success, American Crafts); Misc: Letter Gothic font

Original

This photo of my mother and her sisters was so fun to discover. It's interesting to think how those three little girls became the women I know today. To celebrate and enhance this heritage photo, I chose papers with soft colors and patterns. I also added a simple scalloped edge and a hand-cut flower to further convey the comforting theme of sisterly love.

Supplies: Cardstock; patterned paper, letter stickers, button (Scenic Route); Misc: scalloped punch, Book Antiqua font

Kicked Up!

Because heritage photos aren't always in the best condition, it can be useful to use image-editing software along with digital overlays to further enhance their vintage appearance. I kicked this old photo up a notch with the addition of a vintage overlay and a worn-looking digital frame and then placed the photos on a digital vintage paper. The silk ribbon does double duty by softening the edges of the digital photo and providing texture for the layout.

Supplies: Cardstock; patterned paper, buttons, chipboard letter (Scenic Route); digital frame, overlay, paper by Rhonna Farrer (Two Peas in a Bucket); Misc: scalloped punch, ribbon, Book Antiqua font

Artwork by Angelia Wigginton

Original

Wesley's grandmother knows little ones very well. She purchased this inflatable ball pit to have on hand when he visits—and he loves it! The patterned papers I chose for this layout echo the colors found in the photos, and the prints support the playful theme. Lots of journaling accompanies the single photo.

Supplies: Cardstock; patterned paper (Me & My Big Ideas, Scenic Route, Sassafras); letters (American Crafts); rub-on (Deja Views); Misc: Arial font

Kicked Up!

The original layout is cute, but it needs more—more photos of Wesley in action! The addition of three small photos alongside the focal photo adds joy and action to the layout and supports the story told in the journaling. Instead of just hearing about Wesley playing, you can now see how he played, complete with smiles and laughter.

Supplies: Cardstock; patterned paper (Me & My Big Ideas, KI Memories); letters (American Crafts); rub-ons (Scenic Route); stickers (KI Memories); brads (Making Memories); photo turn (7Gypsies); Misc: Arial font

QUICK TIP

Round two corners of a photo for an unexpected way to frame it.

Original

Some of my favorite memories are those made on our annual family vacation to the beach. The white sand and green grasses provide the perfect backdrop for the special photos I like to take of my daughter Michaela. The soft blues and greens in these papers match the cool, breezy feel of these two photos while the buttons, bow and fabric flowers add girly details.

Supplies: Patterned paper (American Crafts, Chatterbox, BasicGrey, Creative Imaginations); die-cuts, pearls (K&Co.); rub-ons (Creative Imaginations); brackets (American Crafts); flowers, button (Making Memories); ribbon (May Arts); Misc: Times New Roman font

Kicked Up!

The original layout is sweet, and the colors are well chosen, but both photos of Michaela are taken from almost the same distance, and there are distracting elements in the background. I've found that planning how I want to shoot helps me stay focused and get the shots I want in the shortest amount of time. By getting closer to your subject (or cropping the shot afterward), you can highlight your subject and eliminate distractions in the background, as well as provide more personality for the page.

Supplies: Patterned paper (Pink Paislee, Chatterbox, KI Memories); letters, rub-ons (American Crafts); chipboard (American Crafts, Scenic Route); ribbon (May Arts); button (Heidi Swapp); Misc: Times New Roman font

Artwork by Angelia Wigginton

Original

When visiting the beach, I like to watch my two girls as they enjoy the sand and sea. The gray background on this layout allows the light-colored photos to shine. The blue patterned papers and acrylic flower not only enhance the seaside theme, but they coordinate with the colors found in the girls' swimsuits.

Supplies: Cardstock; patterned paper (BasicGrey, Scrap In Style); flower (Making Memories); chipboard button (KI Memories); letters (American Crafts); Misc: buttons, fabric, Times New Roman font

Kicked Up!

The first layout contains the right colors and patterns for a beach layout, but the overall design is basic and a bit choppy, with a title that doesn't fit the journaling. For a more cohesive effect, combine your photos into one large photo block, allowing room for a title across the middle, instead of the usual top or bottom placement. Placing embellishments, like sheer flowers and rings, on the right side balances the heavy photo block.

Supplies: Cardstock; patterned paper (BasicGrey, Scrap In Style); flowers (Making Memories); chipboard buttons (KI Memories); letters (American Crafts, Making Memories); sticker (K&Co.); Misc: fabric, Times New Roman font

Original

Downtown Chicago is one of my favorite places to wander around and take in the sites, shop and people watch. I love snapping photos to document what I see. For this layout, I kept the design simple to feature multiple photos. The colors and patterns of the papers enhance the photos without taking anything away from them, and the black letters and embellishments tie it all together.

Supplies: Patterned paper (Chatterbox, Making Memories, October Afternoon); brads, stickers (Making Memories); chipboard (Chatterbox); Misc: Garamond font

Kicked Up!

The original layout is pretty, but this kicked-up layout boasts a bit more drama, created with photos that are cropped and stretched. By using a unique shape, the subjects in the photos instantly demand attention and become even more the focus of the layout. In addition, the photos take up less space, leaving room for a larger, more embellished title better suited to a dramatic design.

Supplies: Patterned paper (Chatterbox, Making Memories, October Afternoon); brad (Little Yellow Bicycle); chipboard (BasicGrey, Chatterbox); rub-ons (American Crafts); stickers (Carolee's Creations); Misc: pen, Garamond font

Original

I'm so thankful I was able to get a photo of Ashlyn and her friend on their last day of preschool. I wanted to make sure I accurately captured their beautiful little friendship, so I chose some pretty floral papers, a scalloped-edge journaling block and a decorative border to show off the photo. The hand-sewn buttons, stitching and inked edges also help to enhance the cozy feeling of the photo.

Supplies: Cardstock; patterned paper (Sassafras, Scenic Route); stickers (Scrapworks, Sassafras, Scenic Route, Adornit); buttons (BasicGrey); Misc: Tahoma font

Kicked Up!

You know the phrase "you don't know what you're missing"? That's what comes to mind when I compare this layout to the original. While the original layout is lovely, seeing the transparent photo frame on this layout makes me realize what was missing. With glittery flowers and a delicate frame, the photo is transformed into something special, and the lines around the girls' faces are softened to match the feel of the layout.

Supplies: Cardstock; patterned paper (Sassafras, Scenic Route); frame (Fancy Pants); chipboard, buttons (Basic-Grey); rub-ons (October Afternoon); stickers (Sassafras); Misc: ink, Tahoma font

Original

The first snowfall of the season is such a magical time, especially for two eager little girls. For this layout, I chose winter-themed papers in colors that brightened up the mostly white photos. A die-cut snowflake on the main photo adds much-needed visual weight to a lightly colored photo and ties it in with the patterned papers. Finally, small amounts of red accents help the layout spring to life.

Supplies: Cardstock; patterned paper (Deja Views, October Afternoon); die-cut (Provo Craft); chipboard, buttons (BasicGrey); ribbon (Maya Road); rub-on (Scenic Route); Misc: glitter glue, acrylic paint Franklin Gothic Book font

Kicked Up!

Although the original layout shows off the main photo well enough, it really stands out on this page. A circular photo is unexpected, and pairing it with a wavy border gives the layout more energy, which is more reflective of the action in the photos. The main photo seems to float on the page, just like two little girls gliding over the snow. The two large snowflakes enhance the wintry feel while grounding the focal photo.

Supplies: Cardstock (Bazzill); patterned paper (Deja Views, October Afternoon); chipboard (Maya Road, BasicGrey); rub-on (Scenic Route); sticker (Deja Views); buttons (BasicGrey); ribbon (Maya Road); Misc: acrylic paint, glitter, Franklin Gothic Book font

Original

Olivia's summer days are full of her favorite activity: swimming! This photo of her ecstatic, smiling face needed a page of its own. The blue of the water matched the blue of her eyes and provided the color direction for the layout. Accents of scalloped yellow paper strips, orange puffy stickers and green vinyl alphabet stickers are great complements to this "hot" topic.

Supplies: Cardstock; patterned paper (Luxe Designs, KI Memories, Scenic Route, Chatterbox); letters (American Crafts); Misc: circle punch, Berlin Sans FB font

Kicked Up!

Although I love the expression on Olivia's face in the photo, her arm and the ladder in the pool distract from her face on the original layout. I didn't want to crop the photo for this layout and lose the blue of the pool water, as it lent atmosphere to the page, so I employed a creative cover-up technique. Placing my journaling strips over the distractions allowed my daughter's smile to get the attention. A title or an embellishment can also hide distractions tricky to crop away.

Supplies: Cardstock; patterned paper (Scenic Route, Creative Imaginations, Prima, BasicGrey); letters (American Crafts); acrylic star (Heidi Swapp); rub-on (Creative Imaginations); button (KI Memories); Misc: Berlin Sans FB font

Original

Who doesn't love something sugary sweet every now and then? Well, my daughter's idea of now and then is mostly now! I caught her enjoying this oversized lollipop and wanted to document her love of sugar using these photos. I kept the focal photo large and in color while adding a strip of other smaller photos to emphasize the playfulness of the page. A basic title, some black accents and a couple of candy heart stickers finish off the page.

Supplies: Cardstock (Bazzill); patterned paper, stickers (Little Yellow Bicycle); chipboard (Little Yellow Bicycle, BasicGrey); pearls (Queen & Co.); Misc: Tunga font

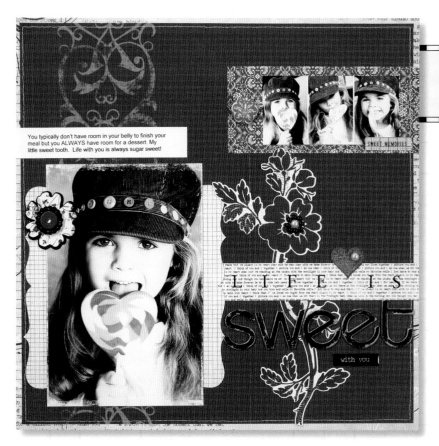

Kicked Up!

While the original layout accurately documents my daughter's love of sweets, all the colors in the photos are a bit overwhelming. So to create a little drama and to focus on the story, I changed the large photo to black and white while keeping the lollipop's color. This change gives the picture pizzazz and adds some flair to the layout.

Supplies: Cardstock (Bazzill); patterned paper, stickers, brad (Little Yellow Bicycle); chipboard (BasicGrey); rub-ons (Deja Views); pearls (Queen & Co.); Misc: Tunga font

I love you more everyday

I've told you before,
I'd do it all over again.
Anywhere with you is home.

20 years

together

Love

Original

sweet

adore

forever

I've told you before, I'd do it all over again. Anywhere with you is home.

YEARS TOGETHER

Home

the best is yet to come

Kicked up!

Chapter 3: Titles

Pick up any newspaper, magazine, book or CD, and you'll notice something they all have in common with our scrapbook pages—titles. Newspapers and magazines have column or article headlines that are meant to capture the reader's interest. Titles on book and CD covers serve as important first impressions. A meaningful title is one of the key components of a scrapbook page, and going beyond the basic, predictable letter sticker titles is what this chapter is all about. Titles can do so much to add pizzazz to a layout. They can tantalize or excite. They can add warmth, glitz or humor. A terrific title can also create a link from the photos to the journaling and help set the mood for the page. Titles can be all shapes and sizes. You can mix products, add dimension and even incorporate paper piecing into your title treatment. Have some fun taking the ideas in this chapter and adding some spice of your own!

Original

I consider myself lucky to have captured these shots of my oldest nephew. He's officially a teenager and, therefore, way too cool to have his photo taken. Choosing a warm brown background and vivid green patterns allows these outdoor photos to take center stage. Spelling Evan's name in chipboard framed by the metal buttons lends a masculine air.

Supplies: Cardstock; patterned paper (Scenic Route, Fancy Pants, October Afternoon, Prima); letters (Prima); buttons (KI Memories); Misc: corner rounder, Times New Roman font

Kicked Up!

One way to grab attention is with a catchy title. Go beyond a simple name and choose a title that says something about the layout you are creating. The journaling on this kicked-up layout focuses on my nephew's age, and the title hints at the story. Encircle your title with metal-rimmed tags, and attach them with buttons or brads for a unique treatment.

Supplies: Patterned paper (Scenic Route, Making Memories, Chatterbox, October Afternoon, KI Memories); letters (Prima); buttons, tags (KI Memories); Misc: Times New Roman font

QUICK TIP

Placing just a small strip of patterned paper alongside photos really packs a punch.

Original

Cruella de Vil was such a hoot when we chatted with her at Disneyland. I love that I captured the moment and my friend's expression perfectly with my photos. I used a bright and bold color palette to further emphasize the fun feeling and a black background to hold it all together.

Supplies: Cardstock; patterned paper, buttons, chipboard, stickers (Scenic Route); Misc: Arial font

Kicked Up!

Although the first layout achieves my purpose of documenting the story, the title is predictable. In contrast, the title on this second layout immediately makes the page come to life. You instantly understand what the page is all about, enticing you to read the story behind it all.

Supplies: Cardstock; patterned paper, buttons, chipboard (Scenic Route); rub-ons (BasicGrey); stickers (EK Success, Scenic Route); tag (Creative Imaginations); Misc: Arial font

Original

My husband delights in making funny faces when he's in front of a camera. Or maybe he just delights in frustrating the photographer! In any case, I've held onto him for 20 years. The colors of this layout lend a lighthearted feel to these photos of us. The red stickers, button and heart add a romantic touch to this sweet layout with a simple sticker title.

Supplies: Cardstock; patterned paper (Fancy Pants, October Afternoon, Scenic Route); letters (American Crafts, BasicGrey); stickers (BasicGrey); rub-ons (Scenic Route); Misc: button, Times New Roman font

Photos by Olivia Wigginton

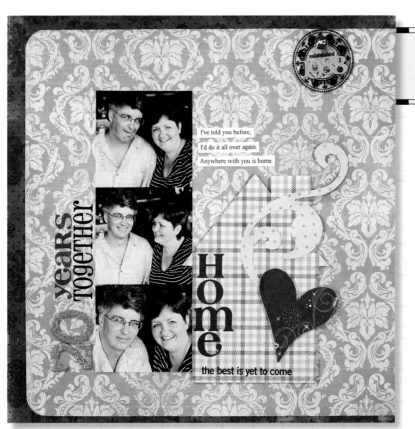

Kicked Up!

Although I really liked the color scheme of the first layout, I felt it needed a bit more depth and richness, especially in the title area. I covered a house-shaped chipboard piece with patterned papers to play up the "Home" title, and I added the title letters and additional accents. Now the title makes more of a statement about our 20 years together and how our home is filled with love.

Supplies: Cardstock; patterned paper (Fancy Pants, October Afternoon); letters (American Crafts, BasicGrey); transparency (Hambly); chipboard (Maya Road); rub-ons (Scenic Route); die-cuts (Fancy Pants); Misc: button, Times New Roman font

Original

Wesley is a little sweetheart with lots of energy to spare. He kept the girls and me entertained during our visit to a friend's home, and we fell in love with him. To highlight these photos, I chose prints in blue, yellow and brown, perfect for a little boy. I also punched circle accents from the patterned paper for added dimension. The title, "Love U," rests inside another circle that offsets the photo and journaling.

Supplies: Cardstock; patterned paper (KI Memories, October Afternoon); letters (American Crafts); rub-ons (Scenic Route)

Kicked Up!

The first layout is a good example of using the patterned papers to guide the design—the paper inspired the circular title and the punched accents. Here, I took the idea to the next level by making the title a bit more special. I layered the title words with various textured circles, adding contrast with lime green details and epoxy brads.

Supplies: Patterned paper (KI Memories, Creative Imaginations, October Afternoon); brads (Making Memories); Misc: circle punches

QUICK TIP
Add instant texture and dimension to punched shapes and die-cuts by crumpling them.

Original

Summertime is full of fun activities and adventures, so I wanted to document all the things that I would miss when it was over. The photos and journaling tell the story of summer so I used a neutral background and limited embellishments for my design. The bold chipboard title adds weight next to the collage of smaller photos and ties it all together.

Supplies: Cardstock; patterned paper, buttons, letters, felt (Fancy Pants); rub-ons, stickers (American Crafts); Misc: Rockwell font

Kicked Up!

The first layout achieves the purpose of documenting my story through photos and journaling. This second layout does all that while adding some pizzazz. Instead of a linear title, I made it curve around a large, playful embellishment. Without distracting from other elements, this technique adds character and whimsy.

Supplies: Cardstock; patterned paper, buttons, letters, felt (Fancy Pants); rub-ons, stickers (American Crafts); brads (Making Memories); Misc: Rockwell font

Original

Marla has captured an important family ritual on this sunny and colorful page. Her collage of photos, journaling strip and mixture of patterned papers tells the story well. However, when it comes to the title, it feels a bit predictable. Although the title tells the readers what to expect from the journaling, the letter stickers are uninspired.

Supplies: Patterned paper (BasicGrey); letters (Polar Bear Press); Misc: pens, Georgia font

Walk team – a daily event in the Kress household especially during the warmer months. The team members leave the house and walk the neighborhood for about an hour. Sometimes they stop at the neighbor's house for a visit, or the bumpy tree for a climb, or the trampoline for a jump, or go for a run in the grass. It's great bonding time for daddy and the kids and when daddy's car comes tearing down the driveway at 5:30 we know that walk team is gearing up to go!

WALK teAm

Starring: Liam, Addy, Daddy and the pups

Walk team – a daily event in the Kress household especially during the warmer months. The team members leave the house and walk the neighborhood for at least an hour. Sometimes they stop at the neighbor's house for a visit, or the bumpy tree for a climb, or the trampoline for a jump, or go for a run in the grass. It's great bonding time for daddy and the kids and when daddy's car comes tearing down the driveway at 5:30 we know that walk team is gearing up to go!

starring liaM*addy DaD*pups

WALK TEAM

Kicked Up!

Marla's first page is well done, but when paired against her second layout, you can certainly see the improvements. By enlarging the title and moving it along a curve at the bottom of the layout, it instantly demands attention and provides movement. The playful white dots on the chipboard letters and the lively subtitle nestled below the journaling provide energy.

Supplies: Patterned paper (BasicGrey); letters (American Crafts, Pressed Petals); Misc: pens, acrylic paint, Georgia font

Artwork by Angelia Wigginton

Original

How often do I get a photo of my girls with all my nieces and nephews? Not often enough. To show off this rare photo, I chose bright colors to match their summer clothing and communicate the happiness they experience when they are all together. The title is a combination of a large rub-on and alphabet stickers. Stickers and butterfly punches provide quick and easy accents to my title.

Supplies: Cardstock; patterned paper (KI Memories, October Afternoon); rub-on, letters (Scenic Route); stickers (KI Memories); Misc: butterfly punch, corner rounder, Times New Roman font

Kicked Up!

To add more dimension and to balance my large photo, I pumped up the title area—literally. Framing a title with a chipboard frame adds detail and weight. Adding label stickers and glittery brads to "hang" the frame completes the dimensional look. Placing a clear butterfly accent beside the title makes for even greater dimension.

Supplies: Cardstock; patterned paper (KI Memories, October Afternoon); rub-on (Scenic Route); butterfly (Heidi Swapp); stickers, brads (KI Memories); letters (American Crafts); labels (Creative Imaginations); frame (Technique Tuesday); Misc: butterfly, corner rounder, Times New Roman font

Original

Looking at these photos makes me long for our casual evening strolls in Rhode Island. Vacations are meant to be relaxing, and these views are exactly that for me. I kept the design for this layout simple so it would not distract from the beauty in the pictures. To contrast with the mainly blue tones in the photos, I added basic orange letters to set off the title.

Supplies: Cardstock; patterned paper, chipboard, button (Scenic Route); Misc: Basic Sans SF font

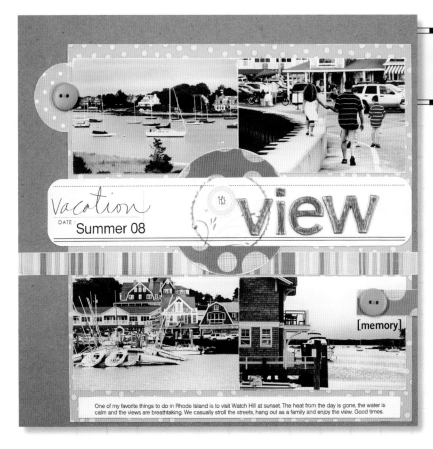

Kicked Up!

Although the first layout conveys the summer feeling, the page feels a bit rigid. I livened it up by making a splash with my title. One great way to do this is to combine digital elements with traditional supplies. Layering digital elements gives the illusion of dimension without adding bulk. The great thing about digital products is that they can be used over and over and customized to fit your needs.

Supplies: Cardstock; patterned paper, chipboard, buttons, rub-ons (Scenic Route); stickers (Scenic Route, EK Success); digital elements by Ali Edwards, Rhonna Farrer (Designer Digitals, Two Peas in a Bucket); Misc: Basic Sans SF font

Original

Denine's son, Ryan, is often hamming it up for the camera, but this time he had a little help from his cousin. Taking her color cues from the beach photos, Denine chose reds and blues for the background, which radiate happiness. Her layered buttons mimic the concentric circles in one of her patterned papers. Her sticker title rests atop her accent photos, with a circular treatment used to match the buttons on her border.

Supplies: Cardstock; patterned paper (BoBunny, My Mind's Eye, Sassafras, Scenic Route); tag (Making Memories); rub-on, sticker (Creative Imaginations); brad (Making Memories); buttons (My Mind's Eye); letters (American Crafts); Misc: pen, floss

Kicked Up!

Although her first layout had lots of happy details, the title didn't reflect the feelings behind her journaling, and it lacked originality. Denine used alphabet stickers in two colors and let her title flow down the side of her layout, generating more energy like that found in her photos. The new wording reminds us to take the time to appreciate the sweet things in life.

Supplies: Cardstock; patterned paper (BoBunny, Sassafras, Scenic Route); brads (Making Memories); buttons (Autumn Leaves); letters (American Crafts); stamp (7Gypsies); Misc: pen, floss

QUICK TIP

Buttons don't have to be boring! Stack buttons or insert brads into them for an unexpected twist.

Original

Michaela has never been afraid to get her hands dirty, and planting pretty flowers is one of her favorite springtime traditions. To support the theme, I chose floral prints in pinks and greens. Matching die-cut stickers make quick and easy photo accents full of color and life. A curly die-cut border sticker along the bottom of the photos balances the title at the top.

Supplies: Cardstock; patterned paper, stickers (BasicGrey); photo corners (Canson); Misc: corner rounder, Arial font

Kicked Up!

The title in the first layout was rather generic, and because of its size, it grabbed a lot of attention. Wanting to focus more on my photos, I chose a smaller title and accented the words with sweet butterflies and flowers. Notice how the photos draw the attention, yet none of the springtime appeal is lost. Keep in mind that big isn't always best.

Supplies: Cardstock; patterned paper, letters, stickers (BasicGrey); rhinestones (K&Co.); flowers (Making Memories); Misc: Arial font

Artwork by Greta Hammond

Original

Although I love something about every season, the transition into fall is one of my favorite times of year. The colors that explode onto the landscape are magnificent, and I wanted to capture a little bit of that on my page. To keep the focus on the photos, I chose patterned papers in fall colors that enhance the hues in my photos but don't overwhelm them. The title is turned vertically and offset with a pair of buttons.

Supplies: Cardstock; patterned paper, buttons (Fancy Pants); stickers (Scenic Route, Adornit); Misc: Times New Roman font

Kicked Up!

A title should not only introduce the story of the photos in words, but in style as well. I felt an elegant title would be more fitting for the beauty found in these photos than the simple and cute title found in the first layout. Using a die-cut title in a formal font, along with more sophisticated words, is an effective and hassle-free way to achieve this look.

Supplies: Cardstock; patterned paper, buttons, die-cut, rub-ons (Fancy Pants); stickers (Scenic Route, Adornit); letters (Provo Craft); stamps (Hero Arts); Misc: twine, ink, Times New Roman font

Original

Thirteen. How did that happen? She's certainly happy about it, as you can see from these birthday photos. Bright green dots and pink flowers decorate this simple birthday page. Applying a large rub-on combined with small felt flowers is a quick and easy way to create a title for any layout.

Supplies: Cardstock; patterned paper (Scenic Route, KI Memories); trim (Doodlebug); flowers (K&Co.); rub-on (Scenic Route); Misc: 2 Peas Fairy Princess font

Kicked Up!

Birthdays at our house are usually loud, happy occasions, and I wanted my layout to reflect that. An additional photo provides for a more complete photo strip, but the bold die-cut title is really what spices up the page. The funky, black number gives the page an edgier, teenage vibe. Accenting the number with a rub-on, glitter brad and circle punches provides instant appeal for my teenager's snazzy birthday layout.

Supplies: Cardstock; patterned paper (Scenic Route, KI Memories); trim, brads (Doodlebug); rub-ons (Scenic Route); title (KI Memories); chipboard (Making Memories); rickrack (Wrights); Misc: 2 Peas Fairy Princess font

Original

It makes me a little teary-eyed knowing these days of dress-up and pretending will eventually come to an end. I'm so glad I took the time to snap some photos of my kids' plan to save the world! The enlarged main photo helps tell the story, while the close-ups bring in the cuteness factor. Black cardstock along with a simple black title plays off the accents in the costumes and works as a solid backdrop for this layout.

Supplies: Cardstock; patterned paper (October Afternoon, Prima, Sandylion); letters (October Afternoon); button (Scenic Route); Misc: pen, Albertus Medium font

Kicked Up!

While the first layout has a clear title, it doesn't accurately portray the playfulness in the photos. In this layout, I kicked it up by layering journaling blocks, rub-ons, letter stickers, buttons and chipboard letters. The dimension and added texture give the title a burst of energy and the arrangement improves the overall flow of the page by drawing the eye up through the layout to the title and photos and then off the page.

Supplies: Cardstock; patterned paper (October Afternoon, Prima, Sandylion); letters, die-cuts (October Afternoon); buttons (Scenic Route); rub-on (American Crafts); stickers (American Crafts, Adornit); Misc: Albertus Medium font

Original

Summer vacations with the family are a magical time for a child. Nic did a great job of capturing the beauty of her family's trip to the beach by selecting a mixture of blue and green papers, which play off her fabulous photos. She achieves a sense of serenity by layering papers and using scalloped edges. A sprig of cut-out leaves connecting the title and journaling finishes the layout nicely.

Supplies: Cardstock; patterned paper, stickers (October Afternoon, Making Memories); chipboard (Cosmo Cricket); Misc: punches, ink, acrylic paint, dimensional medium, Traveling Type font

Kicked Up!

To create a strong title, Nic layered a ring with the mix of letters, giving dimension to her otherwise flat title from the original layout. The ring pulls double duty by grounding the title area and providing a curve for the tiny letter stickers to follow. The chipboard letters provide a 3-D effect, and their glossy treatment carries out the water theme perfectly. All of these elements combined draw you into the layout.

Supplies: Cardstock; patterned paper, stickers (October Afternoon, Making Memories); chipboard (Cosmo Cricket); Misc: punches, ink, acrylic paint, dimensional medium, Traveling Type font

QUICK TIP

Add bling to a title by embellishing chipboard letters with rhinestones. Paint over the gems for a more subtle, but still interesting, look.

Original

There is something so precious about kittens, and Princess is no exception. My girls giggled as the sweet kitten attacked her new mouse toy. The pink and gray papers are feminine and soft, like the small pet, and by using five different small photos, I was able to capture that sense of play. The title spelled out in felt alphabet stickers fits nicely below the journaling.

Supplies: Cardstock; patterned paper (October Afternoon); letters (Making Memories); flowers (Making Memories, Prima); Misc: button, Arial font

Kicked Up!

The first layout is well designed, but the straight lines are too plain for such a playful topic. To kick it up, I added circles of patterned paper and framed a sparkling new title with a sweet scalloped border. For feminine detail, I took advantage of the empty space in my strip of photos and attached a dark pink flower. Changing the basic title to one with more imaginative wording gives the layout additional pizzazz.

Supplies: Cardstock; patterned paper (October Afternoon, My Mind's Eye); letters, brads, heart (Making Memories); frame (Fancy Pants); flower (Bazzill); Misc: button, Arial font

Original

Having two girls, I sometimes forget how active boys can be. That's when my nephews come along to remind me! On this warm summer day, Austin was perfecting his dunking technique. To set the mood and enhance my photos, I chose colors that reminded me of a day spent splashing in the pool. I threw in a water-drop print for added fun, and the bold title words highlight all the action.

Supplies: Patterned paper (Scenic Route, American Crafts, Fancy Pants); buttons, brad (Fancy Pants); letters, brackets (American Crafts); rub-ons (Scenic Route); Misc: 2 Peas Favorite Things font

Kicked Up!

While I took these photos at a pool, they're really more about the action, so I decided to create a page that captured the boyish energy and excitement of the photos. Keeping the blue and orange colors that represent summer, I added large die-cut letters and touches of red for a more edgy, energetic feel. The bold, centered title draws the eye to the photo strip and the journaling sitting atop the photos.

Supplies: Cardstock; patterned paper (Scenic Route, BasicGrey); letters, hearts (Cosmo Cricket); brads (Fancy Pants); acrylic accent (Heidi Swapp); rub-ons (Scenic Route); Misc: ink, Arial font

LIVY

and at 12
she loves
reading
steak
Webkinz
camp
animals
cream soda
tennis
Pokemon
cell phone
lime green

Original

and at 12
she loves
reading
steak
Webkinz
camp
animals
cream soda
tennis
Pokemon
cell phone
lime green

i love livy

Kicked up!

Chapter 4: Embellishments

Life would be pretty boring without all the little extras. Imagine a basic outfit without accessories, cake sans tasty frosting or a blank living room wall. Just like a necklace provides personality, frosting sweetens up a cake and a new piece of art adds flair to a space, embellishments add spice to scrapbook pages. Embellishments aren't required of course—a page can be complete with just a title, photos and journaling. But a layout sure looks better with embellishments attached! Embellishments—everything from flowers and buttons to chipboard and felt—add style and texture and personality to pages. When used correctly, they help convey the story and guide the viewer around the layout. However, with all the different types of products on the market, it's sometimes difficult to know how to effectively use embellishments. In this chapter, we have carved out a few techniques and examples of how to make the most out of the embellishments you use. From handmade and digital to punched out and layered, the embellishments in this chapter are sure to inspire you.

Original

Family is forever, and sometimes in life we get to add a few people along the way. Linda has created this lively page to document the filling of her last in-law vacancy. Her bold color choices complement her linear design and work well with the masculine photos. She kept the paper patterns more subdued to allow her engaging photos to shine, and the small chipboard man icon adds embellishment to complete the title.

Supplies: Cardstock; patterned paper (Scenic Route); chipboard (Technique Tuesday, Maya Road, Deja Views); letters (American Crafts, Cosmo Cricket); nameplate (BasicGrey); Misc: chalk ink, Dream Orphans font

Kicked Up!

Sometimes bigger is better! Linda's oversized man icon hits home the theme of adding that last person to the family. To balance the size of the embellishment, Linda placed a curvy frame around her journaling, which also provides curves against the hard lines. The large icon, with his arm tucked under the photos, and the frame carried over from the journaling bring cohesion that is lacking in the original layout, where the elements are separate.

Supplies: Cardstock; patterned paper, stickers (Scenic Route); chipboard (Technique Tuesday, Scenic Route); letters (American Crafts, Cosmo Cricket); Misc: chalk ink, Dream Orphans font

Original

Although he is an excellent reader, my son doesn't like to admit he can get caught up in a good book. I love how these photos capture an everyday moment around my house. I played up the strong photos with a bold color palette set against a white background. The black title and simple rings accent the page and add some punch.

Supplies: Cardstock; patterned paper (Fancy Pants); stickers (American Crafts); letters (Provo Craft); Misc: circle cutter, Times New Roman font

Kicked Up!

Instead of going generic as I did with the rings on the original layout, give your page a kick by incorporating a themed embellishment. If you can't find one at the craft store, borrow an embellishment from the digital world. I found the adorable bookmark featured on this page in a digital kit; all I did was print it to the size I needed. It adds color, plays up the theme and ties the page together. As a bonus, I can print extras for my son to use in his books!

Supplies: Cardstock; patterned paper, brad (Fancy Pants); digital elements by Danielle Thompson (Two Peas in a Bucket); stickers (American Crafts); Misc: circle cutter, scalloped blade, Times New Roman font

QUICK TIP

Two great sites to find digital kits are www.twopeasinabucket.com and www.designerdigitals.com.

Original

Jennifer's little boy was captivated by a fuzzy caterpillar while out hiking with the family, enjoying nature's fall beauty. Jennifer chose papers to complement her photo, which is rich with greens and browns. In addition, she accented her page with simple details, like a scalloped photo border and a felt-and-paper branch that lends an outdoorsy feel to the page.

Supplies: Cardstock; patterned paper (KI Memories, Cosmo Cricket); letters (Scenic Route); brads (Karen Foster); frame (Chatterbox); bookplate (7Gypsies); die-cuts (Provo Craft); Misc: button, photo corners, circle punch, ink, floss, decorative scissors, Century Gothic font

Kicked Up!

Jennifer was off to a great start with her first page, but this kicked-up layout shows how adding small details can really impact a page. She began by modifying her title, using large corrugated letters that are an unexpected touch. To pump up the volume on her paper piecing, she added additional patterns, inked edges and stitching. She also stitched around the layout. Finally, the darker journaling strips add contrast to highlight the words.

Supplies: Cardstock; patterned paper (KI Memories, Deja Views, Cosmo Cricket); letters (Scenic Route, Deja Views); die-cuts (Provo Craft); brads (Karen Foster); frame (Chatterbox); bookplate (7Gypsies); Misc: button, photo corners, circle punch, floss, ink, decorative scissors, Century Gothic font

Original

Christine has a beautiful scrapbooking style. She always enhances her photos with lovely colors and well-chosen details, and she journals from her heart. On this layout she shares some details about her life right now, using feminine hues and simple butterfly accents hand-cut from a piece of patterned paper.

Supplies: Patterned paper (American Crafts, Collage Press, Pink Paislee, Sassafras, Webster's Pages); letters (Heidi Swapp); Misc: corner rounder, ink, pen, Ali Oops and Helvetica Neue Light fonts

Photos by Greg Drumheller

Kicked Up!

This layout is another great example of how changing small details can make a layout. Christine designed a lovely accent with depth by layering several different products: first a circular piece of transparency with a lovely sentiment, followed by a piece of patterned paper, a clear clock accent, and an acrylic butterfly decked out in rub-ons, paint and rhinestones. Some stitching and a few small circles punched up with adhesive dots finish the page.

Supplies: Patterned paper (Collage Press, Pink Paislee, Sassafras, Webster's Pages); letters, butterfly, rhinestones, clock (Heidi Swapp); rub-ons (Autumn Leaves); transparency (3M); Misc: pens, corner rounder, ink, Ali Oops and Helvetica Neue Light fonts

Photos by Greg Drumheller

Original

While going through old photographs, I was instantly struck by the similarities in these mother-daughter photos, so a layout showcasing the special bonds was in order. These gorgeous floral patterns, along with the flower embellishments, were the perfect choice to enhance the feeling of motherly love. Finally, the two stacked black-and-white photos offset the larger color photo to balance the page.

Supplies: Cardstock; patterned paper (Sassafras); die-cuts (Provo Craft); stickers (Making Memories); pearls (Queen & Co); button (BasicGrey); Misc: tag, Courier New font

Kicked Up!

The flower embellishments in the original layout are pretty, but they fall a bit flat and fail to serve their purpose of enhancing the photos. In this second layout, a little layering, some adhesive dots and ink go a long way to jazz up and give dimension to the simple die-cuts. The new embellishments instantly guide the eye toward the photos, and they stand out on the page.

Supplies: Cardstock; patterned paper (Sassafras); die-cuts (Provo Craft); rub-ons (October Afternoon); stickers (Sassafras, Making Memories); pearls (Queen & Co.) button (BasicGrey); Misc: ink, tag, Courier New font

QUICK TIP

Kicking up flowers is easy! Run a die-cut through an embossing machine and then lightly sand it for added depth.

Original

Olivia loves to plant flowers, but she forgets to water them. I wanted to create a page about her other loves, and I chose soft, romantic colors and patterns to accomplish this. For a quick and easy page, embellish with hand-cut flowers, punched butterflies and scalloped-edge paper that provides sweet detail.

Supplies: Patterned paper (Chatterbox, Scenic Route, Making Memories); sticker, rhinestones (K&Co.); letters (Making Memories); Misc: butterfly punch, 2 Peas Evergreen font

Kicked Up!

Most layouts benefit from the richness that texture and dimension provide, and this layout is a perfect example of how easy adding texture can be. I simply crumpled the hand-cut flowers from the original layout and layered them with crumpled circles. Hand stitching the button centers provides additional detail, and attaching the flowers to chipboard vines brings them to life.

Supplies: Patterned paper (Chatterbox, Scenic Route, Making Memories); stickers, pearls, rhinestones (K&Co.); chipboard (Cosmo Cricket); rub-ons (BasicGrey); letters (Making Memories); Misc: book page, buttons, butterfly punch, 2 Peas Evergreen font

Original

Michaela loves bright, bold colors and patterns, as you can see by her choice of swimsuit. Using her suit as my inspiration, I chose hot summer colors to mix with these beach photos. The beach-themed rub-ons and blue pearls frame my photos and serve as my embellishments and a subtle title treatment.

Supplies: Cardstock; patterned paper (KI Memories, Scenic Route); rub-ons (Scenic Route); pearls (K&Co.); sticker (Collage Press); brad (Making Memories); Misc: Arial font

Kicked Up!

The original layout is nice, but it doesn't fully capture my daughter's bright spirit. Plus, the hard lines make it appear static. Creating movement and enhancing a design doesn't have to be complicated; just repeat similar embellishments around the perimeter of the page as I did. The glittery floral die-cuts and sprinkling of pearls were an easy way to jazz up the original layout. Attaching the die-cuts with adhesive foam adds dimension without distracting from the photos.

Supplies: Cardstock; patterned paper (KI Memories, Sassafras, Scenic Route); rub-ons, chipboard (Scenic Route); glitter die-cuts, pearls (K&Co.); sticker (Collage Press); brads (Doodlebug, Making Memories); Misc: Arial font

Original

We have been to the beach every year since Ashlyn was a baby, but this was the first year she really enjoyed the water. I made sure to capture several pictures and wanted to create a layout documenting the change in her attitude! The blues in the layout coordinate with the water theme, and the touch of red pops the focal photo off the page as well as helps the title to stand out. A single red button and piece of striped paper tie the colors together.

Supplies: Cardstock; patterned paper, button, chipboard (Fancy Pants); stickers (October Afternoon); Misc: Tahoma font

Kicked Up!

While solidly designed, the straight lines and sparse embellishment on the original layout don't match the energy reflected in the photos. Strategically placing three groups of embellishments on this page allows the eye to flow from the top left of the page to the bottom middle and back up to the top right. The curvy shapes of the embellishments all add playfulness and provide instant energy and movement.

Supplies: Cardstock; patterned paper, chipboard, buttons, brad (Fancy Pants); stickers (American Crafts); Misc: Tahoma font

Original

My daughter's personality shines through in these photos, so I couldn't help but pair them up with warm, sunny papers. Her expression in the main photo warms your heart, so I kept that photo large. The simple die-cut swirl and flower embellishments draw the viewer's eye to the photo and journaling lines.

Supplies: Cardstock; patterned paper (Fancy Pants); chipboard (Heidi Swapp); die-cuts (Provo Craft); rub-ons (October Afternoon); Misc: ink, Sylfaen font

Kicked Up!

Although the original layout is well balanced, using colors that match the mood, it was lacking spice. On this layout, I exchanged the flat paper flowers for a bouquet of layered felt flowers topped with buttons. This dimension makes the layout spring to life. Plus, the focal photo pops out even more with an inked photo frame and surrounding stitches.

Supplies: Cardstock; patterned paper (Fancy Pants); chipboard (Heidi Swapp); die-cuts (Provo Craft); felt (Fancy Pants, Creative Imaginations); rub-ons (October Afternoon); Misc: ink, Sylfaen font

Original

Nic created this gorgeous layout in honor of her daughter's birthday celebration destination and her big-girl status. The neutral background gives way to the colorful photos and cluster of embellishments—the two flowers and paper swirl—on the page. Her title is concise and to the point and adds visual weight below her photo.

Supplies: Cardstock; patterned paper (Scenic Route, BasicGrey, Sassafras, My Mind's Eye); letters, flowers (Prima); rub-ons (Pink Paislee); transparency (7Gypsies); brads, jewels (Queen & Co.); Misc: ink, 2 Peas Red Dog font

Kicked Up!

While Nic's original layout includes some nice embellishments, they seem a little disjointed when compared to her arrangement on this layout. Nic layered hand-cut roses and a paper spiral with her floral embellishments from the original layout, providing cohesion. The new arrangement also connects better with the journaling block and the title. Overall, the layering of flowers and leaves, ruffling of papers and more pronounced title provide depth for the layout.

Supplies: Cardstock; patterned paper (Scenic Route, BasicGrey, Sassafras, My Mind's Eye); letters, flowers (Prima); rub-ons (Pink Paislee); transparency (7Gypsies); brads, jewels (Queen & Co.); Misc: ink, 2 Peas Red Dog font

Original

Michaela is often found with some small critter in her hands, as these sweet photos of her show. I chose soft pink and brown patterned papers to warmly accent both the color and black-and-white photos. For the flower treatment, I crumpled and layered die-cut flowers. The braided trim and scalloped edge provide the little details that count.

Supplies: Cardstock; patterned paper (BasicGrey, Making Memories); letters, flowers (Making Memories); trim (BasicGrey); button (KI Memories); Misc: 2 Peas Evergreen font

Kicked Up!

Although the simple details of the first page were feminine and cute, the single flower embellishment was rather generic. With the popularity of critter-themed embellishments, it was easy to find butterflies that better suited the layout. After making my own transparent butterfly embellishments, I attached them to a sparkly new title treatment for added shine and dimension.

Supplies: Cardstock; patterned paper (BasicGrey, Making Memories); letters (Making Memories, BasicGrey, Jenni Bowlin); trim, rickrack (BasicGrey); button (KI Memories); Misc: buttons, transparency, 2 Peas Evergreen font

QUICK TIP
Make your own transparent embellishments by adding rub-ons to transparency scraps and cutting out the designs.

Original

Making the bunny cake is an important part of Easter at our house. Grandma makes sure of that! I chose a soft, pastel color palette to coordinate with the Easter theme while keeping the photos the focus of the page. The background's scalloped edges provide softness to an otherwise linear page.

Supplies: Cardstock; patterned paper, chipboard, stickers (Scenic Route); buttons (Scenic Route, SEI); ribbon (Offray); tag (Creative Imaginations); Misc: punch, Arial font

Kicked Up!

For this kicked-up layout, the simple repetition of one type of embellishment—buttons—captures the readers attention while bringing cohesion to the page. While the first layout displays the photos well and the colors match the mood, it feels rigid. However, the addition of the border of buttons as well as buttons on the picture tags conveys a sweet warmth and richness that were lacking in the original layout.

Supplies: Cardstock; patterned paper, chipboard, stickers (Scenic Route); buttons (Scenic Route, SEI); ribbon (Offray); tag (Creative Imaginations); Misc: punch, Arial font

Original

One of our Halloween traditions is to hit the stores downtown after school for a little scare-free, light-of-day, trick-or-treating. Purely by chance, I caught this photo of my daughter and her friend walking hand in hand down the sidewalk with their pumpkin buckets. It perfectly portrays what this event is about at this age, so I enlarged it and made it front and center on this layout. I added simple details and muted colors to finish the page.

Supplies: Cardstock; patterned paper (Little Yellow Bicycle); buttons (BasicGrey); letters (Deja Views); Misc: Palatino Linotype font

Kicked Up!

The simple patterns and lack of embellishments give little indication of what story the original layout is telling. While subtle is not bad, in comparison to this layout, the original lacks personality. The bright orange background, accents in black and all the Halloween goodies on this layout instantly speak about Halloween. The embellishments invite the viewer in and to linger a while looking at all the details and taking in the story.

Supplies: Cardstock; patterned paper, stickers, ribbon, brad (Little Yellow Bicycle); letters (Little Yellow Bicycle, EK Success); gems (Queen & Co.); Misc: Palatino Linotype font

Original

Scrapbooking has enriched my life in many ways, but the friendships I've formed are truly the best treasures to come from the hobby. I've spent many happy hours talking, laughing and scrapbooking with Janet and JoAnn, so I created a simple page to document the friendship. Taking my color cues from the photos, I chose orange, gray and black patterned papers. For simple accents, I hand-cut flowers from one of the prints.

Supplies: Cardstock; patterned paper (BasicGrey, Scenic Route); letters (Scenic Route, American Crafts); rub-on (Scenic Route); chipboard (Cosmo Cricket); sticker (Me & My Big Ideas); Misc: 2 Peas Evergreen font

Kicked Up!

I really liked the colors and overall design of the original layout, but the graphic look of the page lacked depth and softness. Some simple additions were all I needed to give this layout a girly feel. A few more feminine patterns (in the paper and the flowers) softly frame the photos, while the flowers, attached with wood and metal buttons, create a border that balances the three photos of me and my girlfriends.

Supplies: Cardstock; patterned paper (BasicGrey, October Afternoon); letters (American Crafts); rub-on (Scenic Route); flowers (Making Memories); buttons (KI Memories); Misc: 2 Peas Evergreen font

Original

Many of our hot Mississippi summer days are spent by the pool, and this layout captures one of those days. Drawing color inspiration from your photos is a great way to choose patterns for a layout, so I chose blue and green patterned papers and paper flowers that echo the colors in Michaela's swimsuit. Placing my photos and journaling at an angle gives the layout a little bit of the unexpected.

Supplies: Cardstock, patterned paper (KI Memories, American Crafts, Making Memories); letters (American Crafts); brads (Doodlebug); flowers (Prima); Misc: Berlin Sans FB font

Kicked Up!

Coordination is good, but be careful that you don't create layouts that are too matchy-matchy so that nothing stands out on the page. In the original layout, the colors echo those found in the photos, but the layout lacks contrast. The red embellishments I added to this page match the hot summer theme and add spark and keep the details from fading into the background. They also create a visual triangle to lead the eye around the page.

Supplies: Cardstock; patterned paper (KI Memories, American Crafts, Scenic Route, Making Memories); letters (American Crafts, Doodlebug); ribbon (American Crafts); brads (Doodlebug); stickers, accents (KI Memories); Misc: Berlin Sans FB font

Original

To remind herself of precious moments spent with her son wading in rain puddles, Christine took a photo of his little boots sitting by the door. To highlight this single photograph, she created a large circular photo mat with the edge intersecting her title block. She tucked her journaling underneath her title, hugging the curve of her photo mat. Altogether, the elements create a simple, but pleasing, design.

Supplies: Cardstock; patterned paper (October Afternoon, Prima, Tinkering Ink); button (Autumn Leaves); letters (American Crafts); sticker (Jenni Bowlin); Misc: circle template, ink, pen, AL Postmaster font

Kicked Up!

Loving the circular photo mat but not how the title commanded too much attention, Christine made a few changes to the original layout. First, she added circles down the left side of her layout, which lead the eye right down to the photo. These embellishments also serve to balance the title strip. Christine made her title smaller, but added weight to the area with the circular journaling box, which also serves as an additional embellishment.

Supplies: Cardstock; patterned paper (October Afternoon, Prima, 7Gypsies, American Crafts, BasicGrey, Tinkering Ink); letters (American Crafts); sticker (Jenni Bowlin); photo turn (7Gypsies); stamp (Label Tulip); Misc: pen, circle template, circle punch, ink, AL Postmaster font

Pet exotic

This eyelash gecko, also known as a crested gecko, was definitely one of Austin's more exotic pets. He required a special habitat consisting of bark pieces, rocks for climbing and basking, food and water dishes, and a light. His diet consisted of delightful dried flies, millworms, crickets, and carrots. Yum, yum...NOT.

Original

This eyelash gecko, also known as a crested gecko, was definitely one of Austin's more exotic pets

He required a special habitat consisting of bark pieces, rocks for climbing and basking, food and water dishes, and a light

Austin remembers his gecko's favorite activity was sleeping on a big rock, warming himself under the light above.

His diet consisted of delightful dried flies, millworms, crickets, and carrots. Yum, yum...NOT

He was gentle, liked being held and even tolerated having his tummy rubbed.

eyelash gecko

Kicked up!

Chapter 5: Journaling

Words are powerful. They have the power to make us laugh or cry, to recall emotions, and to move us in many ways. Coupled with music or colors or breathtaking scenery, they make an even bigger impact. Just the same, photos and journaling go together to create a powerful scrapbook page. The right words on a scrapbook page make for a meaningful and lasting memory. And how you say the words—how the journaling is designed—can also make stories more meaningful. This chapter is all about using your journaling to take layouts up a notch. You'll see examples for redesigning your journaling in kicked-up ways, like incorporating stamped images, adding fancy borders or including stickers. Plus get ideas for rewriting the words, journaling with humor and getting others involved in the process. All these ideas can be used again and again to create powerful pages.

Original

Just looking at these photos of my kids wearing their Thanksgiving creations makes me smile. The warm tones and distressed look of the papers help enhance a feel of home and gratitude. I continued that theme with journaling that describes why these little creations were a breath of fresh air and why I am thankful.

Supplies: Cardstock (Bazzill); patterned paper (Pink Paislee); buttons (BasicGrey); stickers (Pink Paislee, American Crafts); Misc: Gautami font

Kicked Up!

The original layout is heartfelt, but I stepped up the homey feeling on this page here. Instead of a boring square journaling box, I printed my journaling onto a bracket label sticker and then attached it to a coordinating chipboard piece. Suddenly, my heartfelt journaling takes on more prominence and appears interesting and more vibrant.

Supplies: Cardstock; patterned paper, chipboard (Pink Paislee); buttons (BasicGrey); stickers (Pink Paislee, American Crafts); Misc: Gautami font

QUICK TIP
Journaling blocks aren't just for handwriting. Line up your text in a word processing program, temporarily adhere journaling block to paper and then run it through your printer.

Original

Grown-ups deserve a little rest and relaxation every now and then! Linda used this layout to celebrate some fun adult drinks she and her family enjoyed aboard a cruise ship. Her blue background mimics water, and the subdued patterns convey the tranquil feeling of being on vacation. The bright green block of color provides a fun place to rest the happy words.

Supplies: Cardstock; patterned paper (October Afternoon); letter stickers (October Afternoon, Pink Paislee, American Crafts); border (Inque Boutique); fabric embellishment (Me & My Big Ideas); button (BasicGrey); Misc: floss, Verdana font

Kicked Up!

There is no rule that says journaling lines must be straight. In fact, Linda's journaling here, which curves around the chipboard wave, provides that extra push to make this kicked-up page really stand out. While the wave and arched journaling give a sense of movement, the patterned paper frame envelops the photos and grounds the layout.

Supplies: Cardstock; patterned paper, chipboard (Pink Paislee); buttons (BasicGrey); stickers (Pink Paislee, American Crafts); Misc: Gautami font

Original

One of the first warm days of the season provided a great opportunity to break out the bubble machine. The bright colors in the photos led me to use a more neutral background and then accent it with shots of color in patterned paper and basic blue journaling blocks. I had instant bubble embellishments by cutting out the circles in patterned paper.

Supplies: Patterned paper, stickers, buttons (Scenic Route); Misc: pen, Tahoma font

Kicked Up!

Admittedly, there are times that making room for journaling on a page can cramp my style. Journaling strips are a quick solution; however, as seen in the original layout, it can also make the layout feel choppy. A great way to solve this problem is to add the journaling right on a photo. The white space in my main photo makes the perfect home for journaling. I was able to save space so I could make the focal photo a bit larger, and the words now feels more connected to the photos.

Supplies: Patterned paper, chipboard, buttons (Scenic Route); letters (Provo Craft); Misc: pen, Tahoma font

Original

This flirty bird patterned paper with its yellow and pink accents just said "Michaela" to me, so it was the perfect addition to this page all about her personality. The journaling notes some of her personality traits, from thoughtful and observant to her joyful, mischievous side. I chose photos I snapped of her on a short vacation and a few simple accents to complement the words.

Supplies: Cardstock; patterned paper (Prima, Fancy Pants, BasicGrey); rub-ons (Scenic Route, Creative Imaginations); die-cut (Heidi Swapp); brads (Doodlebug); Misc: button, Times New Roman font

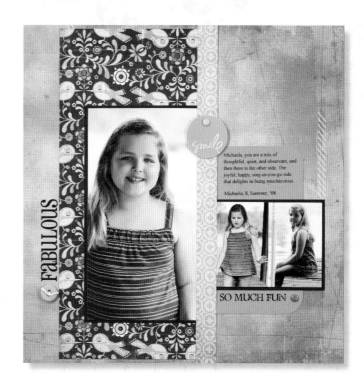

Kicked Up!

As you look at the original layout, you probably notice the journaling is a bit on the light side. For this layout, I chose to journal a lot more. Since the page was all about my daughter's personality, there's a lot to tell! Deeper, more meaningful journaling is an important part of scrapbooking for me. I enlarged my journaling block and used the space to record some of my memories of Michaela during our trip, as well as her individual traits.

Supplies: Cardstock; patterned paper (Scenic Route, BasicGrey); rub-ons (Scenic Route, Creative Imaginations); brads (Doodlebug); stickers (BasicGrey); rhinestone (K&Co.); Misc: button, Times New Roman font

Original

My girls are big on zoos, and visiting this little zoo in Gulf Shores made them very happy. Grouping my small zoo photos in a collage gives them more impact, and I embellished the page with prints that recall our warm, sunny day fun. The brown chipboard accents add dimension and are placed in a visual triangle to highlight the photos and basic journaling about the day.

Supplies: Cardstock; patterned paper (Scenic Route); letters, chipboard (American Crafts); rub-ons (Luxe Designs); epoxy accent (SEI); Misc: corner rounder, Times New Roman font

Kicked Up!

A short block of journaling, like the one on the original layout, works fine for detailing photos, but why not make the page more interactive? To pump up the impact of my small photos, I added specific journaling for each. The numbers on the photos correspond with the fun zoo memories and encourage you to follow along. Adding numbers is easy with rub-ons or stickers, or they can even be added to your digital photos before printing.

Supplies: Cardstock; patterned paper (Scenic Route); letters, chipboard (American Crafts); rub-ons, plastic accent (KI Memories); epoxy accents (SEI); Misc: corner rounder, Times New Roman font

Original

Traveling was a big part of my year in 2008, so I wanted to document in one place all the places I went. I picked some key photos that were both engaging and symbolic of my travels. Because of the number of photos I wanted to display, I used a linear design with minimal embellishments and a neutral background to keep the page from being overcomplicated. I also used bullet points for journaling each travel destination.

Supplies: Cardstock; patterned paper (Chatterbox, American Crafts); chipboard (BasicGrey); stickers (Scenic Route); felt (Chatterbox); Misc: Basic Sans SF font

Kicked Up!

Although the original page is balanced and the colors are a perfect match, the bulleted journaling block feels a little bland. On this kicked-up layout, wrapped the journaling around the title and printed it directly onto the background. Additionally, each line of text begins with the month traveled, which helps the reader follow along. The result feels more connected, with the journaling integrated into the overall design.

Supplies: Cardstock (Bazzill); patterned paper (American Crafts, Chatterbox); chipboard (BasicGrey); numbers (Provo Craft); felt (Chatterbox); Misc: Basic Sans SF font

Original

If there is one thing I have learned to expect, it is to expect the unexpected when it comes to the things that kids say. I don't always understand right away, but I usually do catch up. The journaling on this layout is a case in point. I documented my son's expectations in my journaling and then paired it with photos from his first day of school. These grungy papers complement the colors in the photos, and the simple design allows them to shine.

Supplies: Cardstock; patterned paper (BasicGrey, Sassafras, Imagination Project); stickers (Li'l Davis, Making Memories); button (BasicGrey); Misc: Letter Gothic font

Kicked Up!

While the journaling in the original layout describes the gist of the conversation I had with my son, this second layout goes a step further and relays every word. Providing the actual conversation pulls you into the moment and engages you with the layout. Quotations are a powerful way to communicate on a layout. Kids say the funniest things, so why not use them to your advantage?

Supplies: Cardstock (Bazzill); patterned paper (Basic-Grey, Sassafras, Imagination Project); chipboard (Basic-Grey, Scenic Route); stickers (Mustard Moon, Adornit); rub-ons (October Afternoon); transfer foil (Stix2Anything); buttons (BasicGrey); Misc: Letter Gothic font

Original

Olivia may run from my camera on a normal day, but when she's in the pool, it's all smiles, especially if she can act silly. I chose to take a humorous approach to my journaling to match these goofy photos. Choosing summery prints enhances the summery theme and pool photos. I embellished with paper flowers and glittery brad centers to coordinate with Olivia's swimsuit.

Supplies: Cardstock; patterned paper (Scenic Route, Autumn Leaves, Pink Paislee); letters (American Crafts); flowers (Heidi Swapp, Prima); chipboard (Scenic Route); rhinestones (K&Co.); brads (KI Memories); Misc: Times New Roman font

Kicked Up!

I really wanted the funny story to be the focus, so I chose to make the journaling more prominent on this page than it is on the original layout. I rewrote the journaling to reflect a series of questions that brings the layout to life, and I enhanced the words with stamped circles. I attached the stamped circles with adhesive foam for dimension, creating a border that balances the block of photos.

Supplies: Cardstock; patterned paper (KI Memories, Autumn Leaves, Scenic Route); letters, chipboard (American Crafts); stamp (Studio Calico); rhinestones (K&Co.); clay accent (Li'l Davis); rub-ons (Scenic Route); Misc: Times New Roman font

QUICK TIP

Make quick embellishments by stamping images in different ink colors and punching them out with a circle punch.

Original

We scrappers are usually behind the camera, but it's important to include ourselves in our pages sometimes. Jennifer's idea of documenting what she does and where she does it is great! Her themed paper adds a playful touch, while her scalloped border, chipboard heart and bracket date tab give it a feminine feel. Her straight-from-the-heart journaling is included on strips along the left border.

Supplies: Cardstock; patterned paper (American Crafts, Pebbles, Inc., Die Cuts With A View, KI Memories); date stamp (Staples); button (BasicGrey); brads (Karen Foster); chipboard (Heidi Swapp, American Crafts, Scenic Route); letters (Scenic Route, Doodlebug); label (October Afternoon); Misc: corner rounder, circle punches, ink, decorative scissors, floss, Century Gothic font

Kicked Up!

On the original layout, the simple orange journaling strips add a punch of color. But on this layout, Jennifer took the journaling to a whole other level. Instead of simple strips, she layered words in different fonts and colors for a journaling box that really shows off the words. Her choice of happy colors matches the big smile you see in the photo and communicates the joy she feels in doing her job.

Supplies: Cardstock; patterned paper (American Crafts, Pebbles, Inc., Die Cuts With A View, KI Memories); date stamp (Staples); chipboard (Heidi Swapp, American Crafts, Scenic Route); button (BasicGrey); brads (Karen Foster); letters (Doodlebug); label (October Afternoon); Misc: corner rounder, circle punches, ink, decorative scissors, floss, Hettenschweiller font, Times New Roman font, Century Gothic font

Original

The bold, primary colors together with the red fireman's hat in the photos leave little doubt that this layout is about a boy and his imagination. I loved that I captured these action shots of my son in the midst of his creative play. The black cardstock is the perfect background to set off the wave of color, and the descriptive journaling tells the rest of the story.

Supplies: Cardstock; patterned paper (October Afternoon); chipboard (Heidi Swapp); buttons (BasicGrey); stickers (EK Success, October Afternoon); Misc: Tahoma font

Kicked Up!

Your stories are interesting, and journaling should reflect that! For this layout, I took the dull square box from the original layout and gave it a little life by replacing a few key words with colorful stickers. It provides the playful feeling that I was after and brightens up the page as well. It also draws attention to important words in the story, enhancing the theme.

Supplies: Cardstock (Bazzill); patterned paper (October Afternoon); buttons (BasicGrey); chipboard (Heidi Swapp); stickers (EK Success, October Afternoon); Misc: Tahoma font

Original

Our everyday feelings and moments are so important to capture and describe so we don't forget them. I am treasuring the time I have with my daughter at home before she starts school next year. We have our little routines, and the days go pretty smoothly. These gorgeous papers make the perfect backdrop for these adorable photos. The cut-out hearts, pops of red and sentimental journaling carry out the loveable theme.

Supplies: Cardstock; patterned paper, chipboard, rub-ons, button (Fancy Pants); pearls (Queen & Co.); Misc: Tahoma font

Kicked Up!

Journaling is an important part of documenting our memories, so the pressure can make it easy for us to fall short in providing an accurate portrayal of our feelings. The journaling on the original layout doesn't really capture what I was feeling when I wrote it. Conversely, on this layout, by starting each statement with the same word, the journaling is both interesting and unified. The words take on a rhythm and become a poem of sorts that matches the romantic feel of the page.

Supplies: Cardstock; patterned paper, chipboard, ribbon, buttons, rub-ons (Fancy Pants); stickers (Adorn-it); pearls (Queen & Co.); die-cut (Provo Craft); Misc: floss, Mistral and Script Bold MT fonts

Original

Ever since we visited Austin and his gecko, Olivia has been wishing for one of her own. This little pet captivated her and prompted a trip to the pet store to see more of his kind. The short journaling notes some of the special equipment and supplies need-ed for an exotic pet like this one, while the photos show how easy he is to handle. A simple title and circle accents finish off this quick and easy page.

Supplies: Cardstock; patterned paper (Scenic Route, BasicGrey, Fancy Pants); letters (American Crafts, Making Memories); Misc: 2 Peas Chestnuts font

Kicked Up!

The journaling in the first layout gives some informative details regarding the eyelash gecko, but it's presented in a plain, rather uninteresting block format. In this second layout, the journaling takes a more prominent role in balancing the large photo block and provides more details. Also, by separating the journaling into bulleted points, it makes it easier to read and helps the eye flow down the page.

Supplies: Cardstock; patterned paper (BasicGrey); letters (American Crafts, Making Memories); brads (K&Company); transparency (Hambly); rub-on (Creative Imaginations); Misc: Two Peas Chestnuts font

Original

Michaela will be quick to tell you that she loved her tiger experience. I stood outside the enclosure taking photos of the action—baby tigers falling all over themselves and Michaela trying to stay near. The browns and golds in the patterned paper echo the soft colors found in the photos and match the feel of the warm, sunny day we experienced at the zoo. I topped it off with a simple title and basic journaling describing the photos.

Supplies: Cardstock; patterned paper (BasicGrey, Sassafras, October Afternoon); letters (American Crafts, Sassafras); buttons (Fancy Pants); rub-ons (Creative Imaginations); Misc: book page, 2 Peas Evergreen font

Kicked Up!

I think it's important to include my family in the memory-keeping process. That means I sometimes ask them for their ideas regarding page design, photo, paper and embellishment selection, and also journaling. By including Michaela's own thoughts and feelings on this layout, I created a more personal connection than there is on the original layout. Changing the general title to something Michaela would have said also enhances the page's emotion.

Supplies: Cardstock; patterned paper (Fancy Pants, October Afternoon, Sassafras); brads (Fancy Pants); rub-ons (Creative Imaginations); letters (American Crafts, Sassafras); title (BoBunny); Misc: book page, Two Peas Evergreen font

Original

When my sister asked me to take some photos of my nephews and my niece, little did I know that I'd capture the family dynamics so well. There is Marissa looking so innocent, and Austin doing his best to tease, while Evan looks on. Using the colors in Marissa's blouse, I chose dimensional buttons with similar colors to use against a solid background. A pink print and a block of journaling frame the black-and-white shots, and a simple rub-on title sits on top.

Supplies: Cardstock (Bazzill); patterned paper, rub-ons (Scenic Route); buttons (KI Memories); Times New Roman font

Kicked Up!

Yes, Marissa, you are a princess! After I completed the original layout, I realized that using the large photo of Marissa as my main one called for a page focused more on her, with journaling written from her perspective. Plus, the supporting photos were so funny that the journaling needed to reflect that humor. To top off the new page, I added a playful flower accent that balances the larger photo and anchors the small title strip.

Supplies: Cardstock; patterned paper (BasicGrey, Sassafras); flower, rub-ons (Scenic Route); button (American Crafts); brads (Making Memories); sticker (BasicGrey); Misc: Times New Roman font

snowman

snowball

playing with my c

just having

COL

a perfect snow day

catching some...catching some... catching some... catching some...

air

whOOsh

whOa

You and Daddy catching some air as you fly down
the hill on a gorgeous winter afternoon.

Chapter 6: Gallery

In the previous chapters, you've explored ways to create a layout and pump it up a notch, make it wow and give it that extra-special touch. One by one, you've seen a little of everything, from background design and photography, to title treatments, journaling techniques and embellishments. Each set of before-and-after layouts was designed to inspire, teach and encourage you to have the confidence to take your scrapbooking to the next level. How do we top that? Look ahead to see this chapter filled to the brim with wonderful examples of layouts with spice that incorporate one, two and even three kicked-up elements. You'll find single- and double-page layouts in all different styles from a variety of scrapbookers who never hesitate to **Kick It Up!**

Amelia's layout about her adventure to see the mountain gorillas is one after my own heart. It is simple in design, but yet her intricate embellishments and beautiful line of photos, plus the engaging journaling, make this page anything but simple. She drew me in with her incredible photos and then mesmerized me with her hand-stitched curves and elaborate use of rub-ons and acrylic shapes. The angle on the flowers and trees gently guides your eye from the photos to the title and through to the journaling. This layout is the complete and total package!

Supplies: Cardstock; patterned paper (SEI); acrylic shapes (Heidi Swapp, My Mind's Eye); letters (American Crafts); rub-ons (Autumn Leaves, Heidi Swapp, Making Memories); Misc: floss, MA Fishy font

Artwork by Amelia McIvor

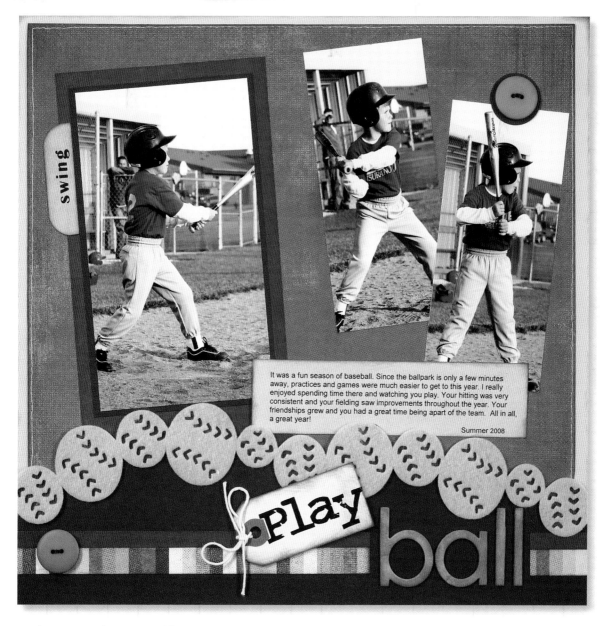

swing

It was a fun season of baseball. Since the ballpark is only a few minutes away, practices and games were much easier to get to this year. I really enjoyed spending time there and watching you play. Your hitting was very consistent and your fielding saw improvements throughout the year. Your friendships grew and you had a great time being apart of the team. All in all, a great year!

Summer 2008

play ball

There is nothing quite like a summer evening at the ballpark. I used natural-colored papers with a grungy feel and minimal patterns to complement the photos of my son at bat. I found the perfect embellishment in this felt baseball border and used it to carry out the baseball theme. Set over a strip of red, the baseball trim is enough to liven up the page without overpowering it.

Supplies: Cardstock; patterned paper (BasicGrey, Crate Paper); baseballs (Queen & Co.); chipboard, button (BasicGrey); rub-ons (Scenic Route); tag (Avery); Misc: ink, Arial font

Artwork by Greta Hammond

QUICK TIP
Brush raw chipboard letters over a brown ink pad to give it that grungey, dirty look great for outdoor pages.

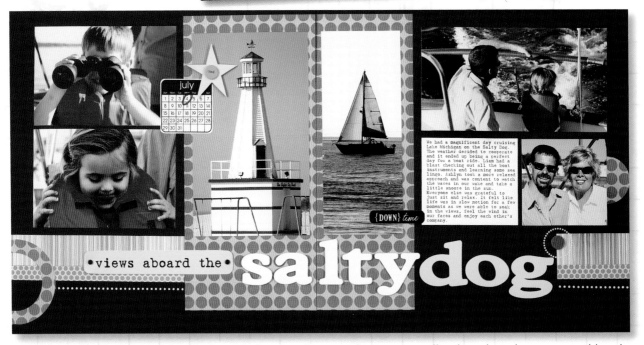

Embellishments don't need to be flashy to enhance a layout. The strategically placed circles, stars and brads on this layout create a visual triangle that effectively guides the viewer's eye across this simply designed layout, from the circle ring in the lower left corner, up to the calendar and star, and back down to the circle, brad and rub-on in the lower right corner. The bold pops of color against the black background provide contrast against the well-composed photographs and linear angles.

Supplies: Cardstock; patterned paper (Scenic Route); letters (Provo Craft, Scenic Route); stickers (Imagination Project); rub-ons (American Crafts); brads (Queen & Co.); Misc: Bastik Regular font

Artwork by Greta Hammond

title

Amy's monochromatic, wintry layout immediately triggers your senses. You can almost feel the cold, wet snow and icy breeze. This is due, in large part, to the unique title treatment. Amy used a masking technique by temporarily placing letter stickers on a transparency, painting around them and then lifting them off. The result? An icy title which is the perfect complement to her wintry theme.

Supplies: Patterned paper (My Mind's Eye); chipboard, ribbon (Fancy Pants); glitter (Tattered Angels); die-cut (Autumn Leaves); lace (Offray); rub-ons (Fancy Pants, Autumn Leaves); stickers (Making Memories, 7Gypsies); brads (Karen Foster); Misc: acrylic paint, pens, correction tape

Artwork by Amy Peterman

time well spent

at thirteen Evan is sometimes distant

not swimming or playing, when Olivia wishes he would.

other times, he is all smiles and fun with her,

and she loves that.

she calls him her "best buddy".

WiTH
you

Born just 11 weeks apart, these two cousins are good friends—most of the time. Using bold patterns that are neither feminine nor masculine, I created a colorful layout that reflects the spice in their relationship. A chipboard frame covered in red gives the focal photo needed attention, while the unexpected bracket shapes kick it up. Plus, the title treatment illustrates that small can still make an impact.

Supplies: Patterned papers (BasicGrey, Making Memories); frame (Jenni Bowlin); rub-ons (Scenic Route, BasicGrey); letters (BasicGrey); buttons (SEI); MIsc: Times New Roman font

Artwork by Angelia Wigginton

I was struck by the sweet innocence of these photos and wanted my layout to reflect that feeling. Using ribbon, rickrack, and tulle, I created an embellishment border that divides my photo block in half and balances my large focal photo. Layering a paper flower, a chipboard embellishment and a beaded pin creates more drama for this "lovable" page, while the strip of smaller photos works well to supports the playful theme.

Supplies: Cardstock; patterned paper (Fancy Pants, Creative Imaginations); chipboard (Fancy Pants); digital frame by Rhonna Farrer (Two Peas in a Bucket); letters (Provo Craft); buttons (Autumn Leaves); gems (Westrim); rub-ons (Die Cuts With A View); word art software (Serif Draw 4.0); Misc: dimensional gloss medium, embossing powder, acrylic paint, Batik Regular font, Times New Roman font

Artwork by Angelia Wigginton

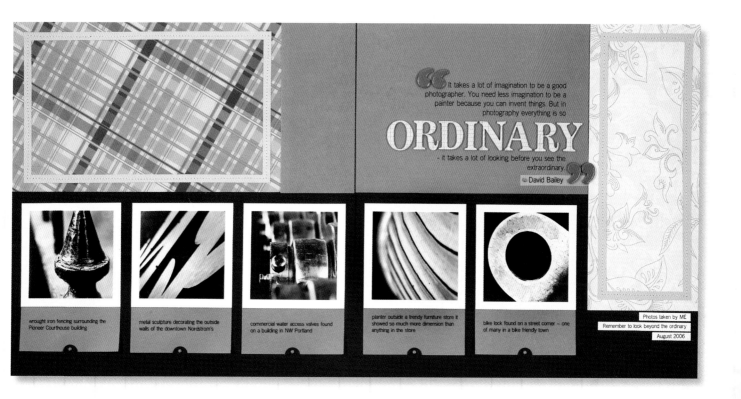

Summer's title might be "Ordinary," but her layout is anything but. Exploring texture and shape and developing her eye as a photographer led her to create this two-page spread. To mimic the shape and feel of a Polaroid, she matted her photos on white cardstock and then added another vellum mat with journaling. As an extra creative touch, she tucked her photo mats into a notch cut into the background cardstock. To kick up the title, Summer embedded the word into the quotation, helping it stand out and adding a creative twist.

Supplies: Cardstock; patterned paper (Fontwerks, Scenic Route); letters (Heidi Swapp); chipboard (Scenic Route); brads (Queen & Co.); Misc: paint, glaze, vellum, Tradition Sans XLight font

Artwork by Summer Fullerton

The words on this layout are what really bring it to life. The tag nestled in the middle of Nancy's journaling draws attention, and the detailed journaling brings humor and warmth to the page about raising children then and now. The soft patterns and colors along with stitching and the scalloped frame add to the homemade feel.

Supplies: Patterned paper, frame (Making Memories); brads (Making Memories, Deja Views); tag (Li'l Davis); flower, heart (Heidi Swapp); clip (K&Co.); label (7Gypsies); letters (Chatterbox)

Artwork by Nancy Damiano

photos, embellishments

Sherry proves that you don't need lots of big photos for a stand-out two-page layout. Although she enlarged one of her favorite shots, Sherry chose eight others and printed them in a smaller format, complete with white borders. With their small size and off-beat placement, the photos act as embellishments and boost the power of the journaling. They also give us a glimpse of her daughter's different moods. Sherry's use of cardstock rings and flower accents in a visual triangle leads the eye across the spread.

Supplies: Patterned paper (Crate Paper, Pink Paislee, Anna Griffin, BasicGrey); flowers (American Crafts, Heidi Swapp); rub-ons (BasicGrey, Chatterbox); brads (American Crafts); Misc: dimensional gloss medium

Artwork by Sherry Steveson

Enthusiasm, motivation, and creativity are all qualities that are necessary to any photographer hoping to capture the personalities of 5 (or more) children of varying ages. Determination, persistence, and patience don't hurt either. I simply asked that they sit on the steps together, and as you can see, I captured lots of personality. And, I wouldn't have it any other way. Evan, 13, Michaela, 8, Marissa, 7, Olivia, 13, and Austin, 11 July, 2008

ENTHUSIASM is excitement with inspiration, motivation, and a pinch of creativity."

Sometimes the outtakes are much better than the "perfect" photos. Looking at these photos makes me laugh, so I chose happy colors and patterns for the page. My lighthearted journaling kicks up the page by explaining the photos and bringing them to life. For a unique and unexpected way to embellish, cut circles from your large photo mat and add scraps of patterned paper behind the cut-out portions.

Supplies: Cardstock; patterned paper (Creative Imaginations, BasicGrey, Fancy Pants); title, chipboard flower (Fancy Pants); flowers (Making Memories); brads (Doodlebug); Misc: Arial font

Artwork by Angelia Wigginton

QUICK TIP
Use oversized pre-printed die-cuts as unique title treatments. Attach with adhesive foam for dimension.

background, embellishments

A 6 hour road trip that kept me laughing the entire time. 'Grease' is the word!

Trying different types of cheeses. Yum!

Visiting the amazing gardens at Keukenhoff.

Staying in a beautiful bed & breakfast, right on the canal.

Walking the cobblestone streets of Edam.

A getaway weekend in Holland with my best girlfriends, it doesn't get any better!

Getaway

Kim had a blast on this trip with her girlfriends, and that joyful spirit is evident in her layout. Her beautiful photos matted with crisp white borders look like professional postcards. To bring attention to her cluster of travel pictures, she encircled them with a large cardstock ring decorated with brightly colored flowers that mimic those found in the photos.

Supplies: Cardstock; patterned paper (Scenic Route); flowers (Prima, Making Memories); buttons (Sassafras); rub-ons, jewels (Imaginese); cutting machine (Xyron); Misc: ink, Script MT Bold font

Artwork by Kim Moreno

This Halloween costume is one of my favorites, and apparently the judges in our town contest felt the same way! Traditional Halloween colors complement the photos perfectly, and this graphic design allows for multiple photos, a fun title and journaling without becoming too crowded. I kicked up the journaling by printing it inside a round journaling spot and then added chipboard, gems and a bow to tie it into the feel of the layout.

Supplies: Cardstock; patterned paper (Scenic Route); die-cut journaling block (Scenic Route); gems (Queen & Co.); chipboard (Scenic Route, BasicGrey); letters (EK Success); rub-ons (Doodlebug); Misc: ribbon, scalloped punch, Arial font

Artwork by Greta Hammond

Little girls love Build-A-Bear, and Olivia is no exception. For her 12th birthday, she invited 2 friends to go shopping, and to visit the Build-A-Bear store in Memphis. There were kitties, monkeys, and turtles, but Olivia still chose a bear!

It is a fact of life: Little girls love stuffed animals! The Build-A-Bear store has all kinds of stuffed animals, but for Olivia, it's bear country. Because the photos were busy, I converted them to black and white, giving them a more classic appeal. I chose whimsical prints to match the warm, fuzzy theme. It's the unusual title shape that makes the layout, adding softness to the strip of photos and leading the eye to the journaling.

Supplies: Cardstock; patterned paper (KI Memories, Sassafras); letters (Sassafras, Pink Paislee); brads (Doodlebug); Misc: circle punch, 2 Peas Evergreen font

Artwork by Angelia Wigginton

I've always considered myself to be a strong woman, one who can roll with the punches and deal with the bumps life brings. Being a military wife for over 14 years indeed puts that to the test.

As a family we have lived in 6 different places, including Germany. We have never owned our own home, always living in base housing. We have worked hard on many yards and houses just to leave them a few short years later. I have said goodbye to wonderful friends knowing that we will likely never live close enough again to visit every day. Having your children crying over missing their friends is a tough thing to swallow. There have been many, many months that I am the sole caregiver to our five small children when daddy has been gone.

There are definite hardships being a military family but those same trials can be considered blessings too. We have been fortunate to have lived in a variety of places. Germany was an amazing experience for us as a family, so many trips to see things we would have never had the opportunity to see otherwise. My kids were exposed to several cultures that will hopefully help them learn to be tolerant of people that maybe a bit different. I have learned that friends become extended family when you are far away from your own. The children make friends easily and have adapted to transitions with ease. As far as playing the single mom for months on end, well that isn't always easy but it has brought me closer to my children and we have all learned a dose of patience.

Jay is nearing retirement from the Air Force within a year. While it will be an adjustment to settle into one house, it will be welcomed. I look forward to us all making friends that will become lifelong friends, planting a garden and watching it grow, and building a house and making it a home. I am that strong woman I have always believed myself to be, it's a good feeling to know.

Kim's paper-pieced house background is charming and the lengthy journaling begs to be read. And it didn't disappoint! Offering descriptions about frequent moves to new places and new homes as a military family, Kim's layout clearly conveys the feeling that "home is where the heart is," which would not have been captured nearly so well without all that heartfelt words.

Supplies: Cardstock; patterned paper (Creative Imaginations, Scenic Route); felt (Jenni Bowlin); chipboard (Basic-Grey); eyelets (Making Memories); embossing (Provo Craft); Misc: ink, punches, floss, Agency FB font

Artwork by Kim Moreno

Extreme Disney enthusiasts are in a class of their own. Nancy admits her obsession in this playful page with an intriguing title that catches your eye. She leads you along with creative journaling blocks of her three Disney confessions lined up at the bottom of the page. Nancy's classic Disney color combination provides the ideal backdrop and sets the tone of the page, and her embellishment touches are small but powerful.

Supplies: Patterned papers (Creative Imaginations, KI Memories, Jenni Bowlin); letters (Heidi Swapp); brads (Deja Views); ribbon (Michaels); tabs (7Gypsies); Misc: locket

Artwork by Nancy Damiano

QUICK TIP
Use humor in your title and journaling to invite readers in and liven up your page.

My daughter kept heading back up the hill after each run, so she must have been having some fun! To enhance the photos, I used a pastel color palette, and a snowflake digital frame kicks up the focal photo. The chipboard swooshes are strategically placed around the main photo to give a sense of movement and energy to this blustery layout. Some curvy word art on the chipboard and around the title enhances the playfulness of the page.

Supplies: Cardstock; patterned paper (Fancy Pants, Creative Imaginations); chipboard (Fancy Pants); digital frame by Rhonna Farrer (Two Peas in a Bucket); letters (Provo Craft); buttons (Autumn Leaves); gems (Westrim); rub-ons (Die Cuts With A View); word art software (Serif Draw 4.0); Misc: dimensional gloss medium, embossing powder, acrylic paint, Batik Regular font, Times New Roman font

Artwork by Greta Hammond

You and Daddy catching some air as you fly down the hill on a gorgeous winter afternoon.

this is the stuff that memories are made of.

summer
blueberries

A quick trip to the blueberry patch yielded three pounds of blueberries and a whole lot of fun! The sun was bright, the picking was easy and the sampling was yummy! Liam prided himself on picking the most berries, I got some fun pictures and Ashlyn enjoyed eating her way back down the row when we decided we were done. All in all, a good day!

This page may be simple, but it's still beyond the basic. Cropping photos to an unexpected shape instantly kicks up the layout. The slices of photographs in this bright, fresh page draw the eye in, and the digital scalloped border is an interesting way to frame the collage. The small bursts of orange pop against the dusty blue background, and the black accents tie the page together.

Supplies: Cardstock; patterned paper (Scenic Route); chipboard (Scenic Route, American Crafts); rub-ons (Scenic Route, Creative Imagination, American Crafts); digital frame by Tia Bennett (Two Peas in a Bucket); buttons (Autumn Leaves); Misc: acrylic paint, Batik font

Artwork by Greta Hammond

Gretchen's big smile says it all—she's thrilled to be running a race with her friends. With its crisp black-and-white color scheme and funky touches of color and bling, Gretchen's layout communicates excitement. Energetic photos call for energetic pages, and Gretchen employed a simple method for kicking up the energy: adding torn edges along brightly colored patterned papers that serve as the background. Finally, large black brackets lead the eye to the journaling strips.

Supplies: Patterned paper (KI Memories); rhinestones, letters (Heidi Swapp); bookplate, brads (Junkitz); die-cuts (Sizzix); rub-ons (Hambly); stickers (EK Success, KI Memories); Misc: ink, Ghostwriter font

Artwork by Gretchen McElveen

background, embellishments

At six, you love exploring the outdoors. You are so observant, spotting birds and squirrels in the trees, and little bits of interest amongst the fall colors.

Happy Beautiful

life is good

love

You picked a small bouquet just for me.
September, 2006

After really hot Mississippi summers, we welcome the fall season—and nature walks—with open arms. To highlight the pictures, I opted for a color-blocked background integrated into the photo collage. Circle punches decorated with flowers and scattered across the page help lead the eye around it. Finally, I layered three pieces of chipboard to create a unique embellishment for the title block of my collage.

Supplies: Patterned paper (Fancy Pants, October Afternoon, BasicGrey); chipboard (Fancy Pants, Scenic Route); brads (Making Memories); Misc: book page, 2 Peas Chestnuts font

Artwork by Angelia Wigginton

FOURTH of

JULY

NICO

age: 3

@ the Coffman's

We spent the 4th of July at the Coffman's new house. They have a great wooded backyard perfect for a picnic. It was mostly a rainy, muggy holiday weekend & we lucked out with the best day weather wise.

The food was really good. I made a delicious tomato pie (for the 1st time). The kids had fun splashing in the baby pool and before we knew it they were dunking their heads and were SOAKED. Sneaky little stinkers! At dusk, Pat broke out the (illegal) fireworks & we lit them up. We won a "parent of the year award" when we handed the kids sparklers & they both proceeded to burn their little hands. Sorry kiddies! Nico loved the fireworks. He kept asking, "what's that noise Mommy?" It started to rain so we said our goodbyes..til next year!

of thee sweet land of liberty

Nancy has a talent for taking typical family photos and creating a page that is anything but typical. Her collage of photos, complete with distressed edges, gives you a glimpse into their fun holiday celebration, and her detailed journaling relays the highlights of their day. The way the largest photo overlaps her journaling block, the machine-stitched details and metal finishing touches draw you into the story and add charm to this Fourth of July layout.

Supplies: Patterned paper (Scenic Route, October Afternoon); ribbon, brads (Creative Imaginations); pocket (Making Memories); paper clip (Doodlebug); letters (Paper Bliss); number (Heidi Swapp)

Artwork by Nancy Damiano

photos

You wouldn't think that tiny photos could make such an impact, but they do! The little photos on Kim's layout about her dad are like little bits of love. Each one shows her father doing something he loved and really makes a statement. Her title expresses her feelings now that he's gone, while her color scheme is masculine, yet warm. The oversized heart-shaped die-cut draws attention to her focal photo, while further enhancing her theme.

Supplies: Cardstock; patterned paper (Cosmo Cricket); stickers (Polar Bear Press); chipboard (Heidi Swapp); rub-ons (BasicGrey); photo turns, brads (7Gypsies); Misc: ink

Artwork by Kim Moreno

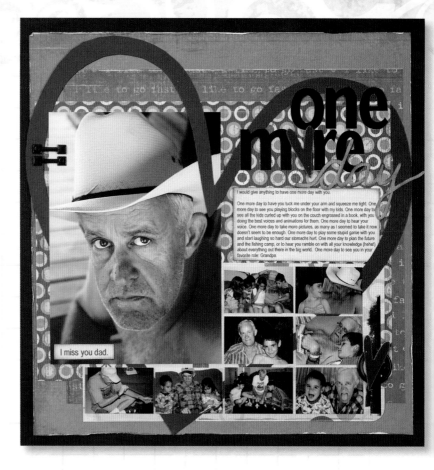

background

Lovers of all things pink will find Cari's layout irresistible. Cari showcases her photos with a background full of shabby chic details like distressing and inking. She also uses lots of texture and a great big background bow, and her two close-up photographs support the full shot of the bicycle. Her layout brings to mind a present just waiting to be opened.

Supplies: Patterned paper (Sassafras, Making Memories); ribbon (May Arts); flowers (Making Memories); letters (Making Memories, SEI); stamp (Bad Girls); brads (Creative Imaginations, Prima Marketing); stickers (Mark Richards, Sassafras); pearls (Mark Richards)

Artwork by Cari Fennell

Gretchen captures the fun of a big family gathering with her happy color scheme of blue and red. Her title, reminiscent of a magazine article, entices you to read on. Gretchen's journaling, though, is what makes this layout a standout. Incorporating numbers into her photo collage is a creative twist, and ties the title, photos and journaling together into one awesome layout.

Supplies: Patterned paper (KI Memories, Making Memories); chipboard (Heidi Swapp); die-cuts (Quickutz); stickers (American Crafts); Misc: pen, circle punch, My Type of Font font

Artwork by Gretchen McElveen

snowman building
sledding
snowball fights
playing with my cousins
just having snow

COLD

a perfect snow day

WINTER

Here in Mississippi, any snow day is a perfect snow day because we get so few of them. Icy blue and white as well as sunshine yellow enhance these cold-weather photos of my nephew. The embellishments on this page—layers of glittery snowflakes with chipboard stars mixed with rub-on snowflakes and rhinestones—add lots of spice. A felt word found in a craft store for the title overlaps the photo block and brings both dimension and texture to the layout.

Supplies: Cardstock; patterned paper (Fancy Pants); rub-ons (Scenic Route, BasicGrey); stickers (EK Success); chipboard (Imagination Project); brad (Doodlebug); rhinestones (K&Co.); Misc: felt, corner rounder, 2 Peas Evergreen font

Artwork by Angelia Wigginton

title

Suddenly, through birthing a daughter, a woman finds herself face to face not only with an infant, a little girl, a woman-to-be, but also with her own unresolved conflicts from the past and her hopes and dreams for the future.... As though experiencing an earthquake, mothers of daughters may find their lives shifted, their deep feelings unearthed, the balance struck in all relationships once again off kilter.
● Elizabeth Debold & Idelisse Malave

3 genera-tions

● Diana Leslie Dafoe photo 1948
● Summer Ingrid Schmitt photo 1971
● Corinne Bready Fullerton photo 2000

Summer's heritage layout is eye-catching for several reasons. First, who can resist an adorable baby—or three? Plus, Summer's use of color gives this layout a very modern appeal despite the vintage photos. Most importantly, the clock, crafted with embossing, chipboard and brads, helps create a striking, original title, which speaks of numbers and time, matching the layout's theme.

Supplies: Cardstock; patterned paper (KI Memories, My Mind's Eye, Inque Boutique); chipboard (BasicGrey, Technique Tuesday); letters (American Crafts, Making Memories); rhinestones (Kaizer Craft); stamp (Inque Boutique); brad (Creative Imaginations); Misc: paint, embossing powder, embossing ink, Traveling Typewriter font

Artwork by Summer Fullerton

embellishments, title

My son was over-the-moon excited when he received an iPod for his birthday. I wanted to document this newfound obsession with a page using a graphic, tech feel. I created my own embellishment with layers of circles and rings that resemble the face of an iPod. These circles bring curves to an otherwise linear page and create a visual triangle of embellishments that guide the eye through it. The creative title posing a question draws the viewer into the page.

Supplies: Cardstock; patterned paper (BasicGrey, Crate Paper); letters (American Crafts, Scenic Route); rub-ons (Scenic Route); buttons (BasicGrey); Misc: Arial font

Artwork by Greta Hammond

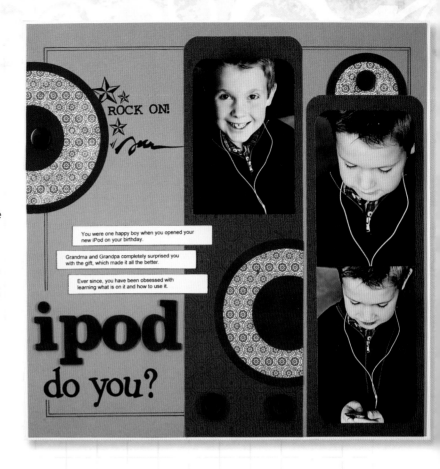

photos

Getting a good family photo proves to be difficult these days, so I was excited to finally get everyone to cooperate. I wanted to create a unique backdrop for this photo, so I turned to my digital supplies. I added vintage digital frames around the photos, positioned them on a digital paper and added digi photo turns before printing everything out. I was able to fill my need for texture by placing this digital printout onto a background of patterned papers and surrounding it with lovely embellishments.

Supplies: Cardstock; patterned paper (Chatterbox, Crate Paper); digital frames, paper by Rhonna Farrer (Two Peas in a Bucket); digital photo turn (Shabby Princess); flower, chipboard, brads (Chatterbox); pearls (Queen & Co.); journaling card (Fancy Pants); Misc.: ink, twine, Book Antiqua font

Artwork by Greta Hammond

Just like my daughter, these photos are sweet, vibrant, fashionable and playful. For this two-page layout, I used a basic black background to set the stage for lots of glitz and glam. From silver rub-ons to rhinestone flourishes to pink felt flowers, this page is loaded with girly touches. It also sports an extra-large title that grabs the reader's attention and makes a statement. Printing the journaling directly onto a coordinating die-cut gives the page added flair.

Supplies: Cardstock; patterned paper, chipboard, letters (Pink Paislee); number (Provo Craft); flowers, ribbon (Maya Road); flourishes (Me & My Big Ideas); rhinestones (Queen & Co.) rub-ons (Pink Paislee, Die Cuts With A View); button (BasicGrey); Misc: Bradley Hand font

Artwork by Greta Hammond

Even without store-bought birthday emebllishments, you know this is a little girl's birthday from the moment you look at this layout. Nancy's precious photos of her goddaughter's birthday party, teamed up with the adorable handmade banner at the top of the page, tell the story completely and make for a page that pops. The wave of pinks and pastels and scalloped edges prove to be a delightful backdrop for this sweet page.

Supplies: Cardstock (Bazzill); patterned paper (Making Memories, Bo Bunny); ribbon (Basic-Grey); buttons (My Mind's Eye); flower (Doodlebug); chipboard (Making Memories)

Artwork by Nancy Damiano

title

You can count on my girls to be jolly on Christmas Eve, as well as excited, loud and silly. To capture that silly spirit, I chose a pink snowflake pattern and mixed in a colorful stripe and some lime green. The stack of brightly colored packages and themed word stickers add to the Christmas feeling. My favorite touch is the glittery chipboard sticker that serves as the title. Layered over a fanciful journaling block, it's a simple but unexpected way to set the scene.

Supplies: Cardstock; patterned paper (October Afternoon, Scenic Route, Fancy Pants); chipboard (K&Co.); stickers (October Afternoon); brads (Doodlebug); die-cut (My Mind's Eye); Misc: 2 Peas Evergreen font

Artwork by Angelia Wigginton

Cari did a beautiful job setting the stage on this page. To enhance her flower photo, she created a paper "garden" on her background. Lacy die-cut flowers, sprigs of bling, buttons and perfectly placed touches of color add a romantic, textured feel to her page. She also layered her background paper and framed her elements to create a shadow box effect—as if she were framing a beautiful memory.

Supplies: Cardstock; patterned paper, crystals, stamp, flowers (Prima); buttons (Autumn Leaves)

Artwork by Cari Fennell

It's not about the perfect photo or the special holidays. It's about being there day in and day out. It's about wrestling on the living room floor and playing in the sandbox. It's about teaching instead of just doing. It's about giving baths and reading bedtime stories. It's about being an example and spending time together. It's about showing your love in all the little ways. It's about the everyday. Everyday things. Everyday life. Being an everyday dad.

everyday DAD

My husband has demonstrated over and over again that he is here for our kids every day, doing everyday things. This page shows that photos can be simple and still stand out. Rather than squish standard-sized photos onto the page, I cropped all the photos to the same size and then displayed them in a collage format. I turned some of them to black and white to help keep the distractions to a minimum. I balanced the large photo section with a long title and journaling box and used bursts of red to add a little character.

Supplies: Cardstock (Bazzill); patterned paper, chipboard, buttons (Fancy Pants); rub-ons (American Crafts, Fancy Pants); letters (Provo Craft); brads (American Crafts); Misc: paint, Arial font

Artwork by Greta Hammond

background, embellishments

Liana has a knack for mixing products that don't necessarily match but still work well together as on this expressive travel page. Her use of layering, from the background up to the photos, is both unusual and intriguing. Cutting out an oversized flower from patterned paper makes for a custom embellishment with a strong impact. Black accents help to ground this colorful layout.

Supplies: Cardstock; patterned paper (Scenic Route, SEI, We R Memory Keepers); rub-ons (BasicGrey, Scenic Route, SEI); paper trim (Doodlebug); stamp (Stampin' Up); epoxy sticker (SEI); journaling tab (Heidi Swapp); digital transparency (Two Peas in a Bucket); rhinestone (KI Memories); Misc: acrylic paints, crayon, paper clip, black pen, glitter glue

Artwork by Liana Suwandi

photos, title

This little scooter has to compete with a Wii system as Olivia's favorite Christmas gift, but she has said many times that she loves it. To add some pizzazz to the basic design, I cropped the photos into slices. I also turned the title on its side to take it up a notch, and I sandwiched the word between the photos. Colorful rub-ons, ribbon and metal-rimmed tags accent this "kewl" page.

Supplies: Cardstock; patterned paper (Fancy Pants, Basic-Grey); letters (Scenic Route); rub-ons (KI Memories, Fancy Pants); tags (K&Co.); brads (Fancy Pants); letters (Basic-Grey); ribbon (SEI); Misc: 2 Peas Composition font

Artwork by Angelia Wigginton

Kids love those pint-sized rides where they can "drive," and from the looks of these photos Nico is no exception! Nancy's two-page spread allows for plenty of photos. A metal-rimmed tag makes for a creative, unexpected photo frame. But the page's extra-=large title, complete with paint and dimensional gloss medium, really takes the layout to the next level. Beyond the basic, it's the perfect complement to the collection of photos because it doesn't get lost on the page.

Supplies: Patterned paper (My Mind's Eye); letters (BasicGrey, Creative Imaginations); flourishes (Fancy Pants); photo corner, stars (Heidi Swapp); photo turn (7Gypsies); buttons (EK Success); ribbon (Michaels): Misc: paint

Artwork by Nancy Damiano

A splash park visit is a great way to beat the heat. On this layout, Nancy captured the fun and vibrancy found in the photos with a bold color scheme and playful embellishments. She offset the predictable lines of a multiple-photo layout with a curved journaling block and a curlicue ribbon trim. Her title and strip of photos, kicked up with epoxy stickers, along with the fuzzy Elmo embellishment provide texture and play up the theme.

Supplies: Cardstock (Bazzill); patterned paper (My Mind's Eye, Jenni Bowlin); letters (Making Memories); chipboard (Scenic Route); sticker (Jolee's Boutique); tape (Heidi Swapp); ribbon (Creative Café); water droplets (Cloud 9 Design)

Artwork by Nancy Damiano

The Birds of the Outback is such a fun interactive exhibit. The enclosed aviary is filled with free-flying cockatiels, parakeets and rosellas. The birds are so colorful and loud! We tried to entice them onto our millet seeded sticks and hoped they would stay a while.

for the BIRDS

Liam was able to lure a few birds onto his stick and then watched them feed right out of his hand! So cool!

I love that I was able to capture a few photos of my son's feathered friends. For this page, I kept the colors and patterns subdued for a natural feel. I gained inspiration for an embellishment from my photos and added a simple hand-drawn tree branch with leaves. I finished it off by perching a couple of felt birds on the branches. Handmade doesn't mean complicated, and easy doesn't mean blah! This simple branch is unique and adds a creative touch to tie the layout together.

Supplies: Cardstock; patterned paper, birds, buttons, letters, journaling block (Chatterbox); Misc: ink, Palatino Linotype font

Artwork by Greta Hammond

Creative Team

Christine Drumheller

Christine lives in Michigan with her husband, Greg, and their two boys, Nate and Zach. She started scrapbooking after the birth of her first child and has been hooked ever since. She has a background in graphic design and a love for typography. She is a traditional "paper and glue" scrapper, and most early mornings, while the house is still quiet, she can be found standing at her scrap desk drinking coffee and playing with pretty paper. She is on the design team for Cocoa Daisy and has been published in several magazines and idea books. She is thrilled to be a 2009 Memory Makers Master.

Jennifer Gallacher

As a designer, writer and teacher in the scrapbooking industry for 10 years, Jennifer enjoys the creative process of preserving important memories. Her designs have been published in multiple magazines and idea books. She serves as a designer for companies including Little Yellow Bicycle, Karen Foster Design and www.twopeasinabucket.com. She has enjoyed creating layouts, cards, and altered projects for catalogs, Web sites, and educational purposes. In addition to her publications, she has served as an instructor for CKU, Nth Degree (an online webcast) and her local scrapbook stores. In her spare time, she loves reading, playing board games with her children and going out with her husband. They currently reside in Utah and love living near the beautiful mountains.

Linda Harrison

Linda's love for design, color, photography and storytelling all unite to form her passion for scrapbooking and paper crafting. Linda has been creating in some form or another since she was a child. In 2005 she took her creating to another level when she began doing freelance work in the craft industry. She has since designed for a variety of manufacturers and has had her work published in several publications. In addition to being the author of *Starting Points*, an idea book published by Memory Makers, Linda was featured as a Scrapbook Trends Trendsetter for 2006, was inducted into the 2007 Creating Keepsakes Hall of Fame and currently serves as a designer for *Scrapbook and Cards Today*. When she's not creating, Linda enjoys filling her days with fun family times with her husband and son, reading, and enjoying the beaches in her hometown of Sarasota, Florida.

Nic Howard

Nic has been a scrapbooker for nearly 10 years. She lives in New Zealand with her husband and three children. She has blue tabs littering every corner of her home and small handmade paper items in every nook and cranny of the house. Nic finds joy in the small things that used to pass her by and has her camera ready to photograph them. Nic's first large scrapbooking achievement was becoming a 2005 Memory Makers Master. Since then Nic has been found in numerous international books and magazines as well as in advertising and galleries of the manufacturers she works for. Nic recently joined the teaching staff at Big Picture Scrapbooking and Prima Marketing. To date, Nic's largest and most fulfilling accomplishment is the completion of her book, *That's Life* (Memory Makers, 2007). It was through writing this book she learned to appreciate the little things that make her an enthusiastic scrapbooker. Those blue tabs she mentioned? Yep, they even gained a page of their own. It's amazing what defines us if we really look around.

Marla Kress

Marla is chief meal cooker, laundry folder, dishwasher, boo boo kisser, diaper changer, book reader, block builder, pretend player, bear hugger and laugh getter to one crazy husband and three small kiddos (yikes!). When she's not on duty, she likes to spend time in her studio creating scrapbook pages, flower pins, hair clips, cards, frames, albums and whatever else her friends and family can enjoy. Marla also loves photography and dreams of being a fabulous seamstress someday (oh, the wardrobe her daughter could have!). Her life as a stay-at-home mom is nothing short of interesting, and she wouldn't trade it for anything in the world.

Denine Zielinski

Denine has been scrapbooking since the birth of her son in 1999. She sees scrapbooking not only as a way to document her memories, but as a much needed creative outlet. She has had her work published in several major scrapbooking magazines including *Creating Keepsakes, Scrapbooks, Etc, Memory Makers* and *Simple Scrapbooks*. She also had the pleasure of contributing to several other wonderful Memory Makers ideas books. Denine had the honor of being named a finalist in the 2006 Memory Makers Masters contest, and she was named a 2008 CK Hall of Fame winner. She is a single mom and an eighth grade civics teacher. She currently resides in Pennsylvania with her nine-year-old son, Ryan.

Source Guide

The following companies manufacture products featured in this book. Please check your local retailers to find these materials, or go to a company's Web site for the latest product. In addition, we have made every attempt to properly credit the items mentioned in this book. We apologize to any company that we have listed incorrectly, and we would appreciate hearing from you. Special thanks to companies that generously donated product toward the creation of artwork in the book (noted by an asterisk).

3M
(888) 364-3577
www.3m.com

7Gypsies*
(877) 749-7797
www.sevengypsies.com

Adornit/Carolee's Creations
(435) 563-1100
www.adornit.com

American Crafts*
(801) 226-0747
www.americancrafts.com

Anna Griffin, Inc.
(888) 817-8170
www.annagriffin.com

Autumn Leaves
(800) 588-6707
www.autumnleaves.com

Avery Dennison Corporation
(800) 462-8379
www.avery.com

BasicGrey
(801) 544-1116
www.basicgrey.com

Bazzill Basics Paper
(480) 558-8557
www.bazzillbasics.com

Berwick Offray, LLC
(800) 237-9425
www.offray.com

BoBunny Press
(801) 771-4010
www.bobunny.com

Canson, Inc.
(800) 628-9283
www.canson-us.com

Carolee's Creations - see Adornit

Chatterbox, Inc.
(208) 461-5077
www.chatterboxinc.com

Chronicle Books
(800) 722-6657
www.chroniclebooks.com

Cloud 9 Design
(866) 348-5661
www.cloud9design.biz

Collage Press
(435) 676-2039
www.collagepress.com

Cosmo Cricket
(800) 852-8810
www.cosmocricket.com

Crate Paper
(801) 798-8996
www.cratepaper.com

Creative Imaginations
(800) 942-6487
www.cigift.com

Daisy D's Paper Company
(888) 601-8955
www.daisydspaper.com

Dèjá Views/C-Thru Ruler
(800) 243-0303
www.dejaviews.com

Designer Digitals
www.designerdigitals.com

Die Cuts With A View
(801) 224-6766
www.diecutswithaview.com

Doodlebug Design Inc.
(877) 800-9190
www.doodlebug.ws

EK Success, Ltd.
www.eksuccess.com

Fancy Pants Designs, LLC*
(801) 779-3212
www.fancypantsdesigns.com

Fontwerks
(604) 942-3105
www.fontwerks.com

Hambly Screenprints
(800) 707-0977
www.hamblyscreenprints.com

Heidi Swapp/Advantus
Corporation
(904) 482-0092
www.heidiswapp.com

Hero Arts Rubber Stamps, Inc.
(800) 822-4376
www.heroarts.com

Hot Off The Press, Inc.
(800) 227-9595
www.b2b.hotp.com

Imagination Project, Inc.
www.imaginationproject.com

Imaginisce
(801) 908-8111
www.imaginisce.com

Inque Boutique Inc.
www.inqueboutique.com

Jenni Bowlin
www.jennibowlin.com

Jillibean Soup*
(888) 212-1177
www.jillibean-soup.com

JunKitz - no longer in business

K&Company*
(888) 244-2083
www.kandcompany.com

Kaiser Craft
www.kaisercraft.net/

Karen Foster Design
(801) 451-9779
www.karenfosterdesign.com

KI Memories
(972) 243-5595
www.kimemories.com

Label Tulip
www.labeltulip.com/

Li'l Davis Designs
(480) 223-0080
www.lildavisdesigns.com

Little Yellow Bicycle* - see Dèjá Views

Luxe Designs
(972) 573-2120
www.luxedesigns.com

Making Memories*
(801) 294-0430
www.makingmemories.com

Mark Richards Enterprises, Inc.
(888) 901-0091
www.markrichardsusa.com

May Arts
www.mayarts.com

Maya Road, LLC
(877) 427-7764
www.mayaroad.com

Me & My Big Ideas
(949) 583-2065
www.meandmybigideas.com

Michaels Arts & Crafts
www.michaels.com

Mustard Moon
(763) 493-5157
www.mustardmoon.com

My Mind's Eye, Inc.
(800) 665-5116
www.mymindseye.com

October Afternoon*
www.octoberafternoon.com

Offray- see Berwick Offray, LLC

Paper Bliss - source not available

Pebbles Inc.
(800) 438-8153
www.pebblesinc.com

Pink Martini Designs - no source available

Pink Paislee*
(816) 729-6124
www.pinkpaislee.com

Polar Bear Press - no source available

Pressed Petals
(801) 224-6766
www.pressedpetals.com

Prima Marketing, Inc.
(909) 627-5532
www.primamarketinginc.com

Provo Craft
(800) 937-7686
www.provocraft.com

Queen & Co.
(858) 613-7858
www.queenandcompany.com

QuicKutz, Inc.
(888) 702-1146
www.quickutz.com

Rusty Pickle
(801) 746-1045
www.rustypickle.com

Sandylion Sticker Designs
(800) 387-4215
www.sandylion.com

Sassafras Lass*
(801) 269-1331
www.sassafraslass.com

Scenic Route Paper Co.*
(801) 542-8071
www.scenicroutepaper.com

Scrap In Style TV
www.sistvboutique.com

Scrapworks, LLC
(801) 363-1010
www.scrapworks.com

SEI, Inc.
(800) 333-3279
www.shopsei.com

Shabby Princess
www.shabbyprincess.com

Sizzix
(877) 355-4766
www.sizzix.com

Stampin' Up!
(800) 782-6787
www.stampinup.com

Staples, Inc.
www.staples.com

Stemma/Masterpiece Studios
www.masterpiecestudios.com

Stix2Anything
www.stix2.co.uk

Studio Calico*
www.studiocalico.com

Tattered Angels
www.mytatteredangels.com

Technique Tuesday, LLC
(503) 644-4073
www.techniquetuesday.com

Tinkering Ink
(877) 727-2784
www.tinkeringink.com

Two Peas in a Bucket
(888) 896-7327
www.twopeasinabucket.com

We R Memory Keepers, Inc.
(801) 539-5000
www.weronthenet.com

Webster's Pages/Webster Fine Art
Limited
(800) 543-6104
www.websterspages.com

Westrim Crafts
(800) 727-2727
www.creativityinc.com

Wrights Ribbon Accents
(877) 597-4448
www.wrights.com

Xyron
(800) 793-3523
www.xyron.com

Index

B-C

Backgrounds 8-21
  combined patterns 13, 15, 18, 20-21
  hand-cut 10, 19-21
  paper-pieced 13, 17
  punched design 14
  scalloped edge 11, 13
Borders
  punched 11, 100
  wave 20-21
Chipboard
  covering with foil 12, 17
  covering with glitter and
    paint 104
  covering with paper 105
Conversations 80

D-E

Decorative edges 11
Die-cuts 60, 64, 66
  embossed 60
  titles 48, 53
Digital embellishments 57
Digital photo mats and frames
  25-27, 104-105, 112
Digital titles 45
Embellishments 54-71
  adding texture to 60-61, 64, 69
  die-cuts 60, 64, 66
  digital 57
  embellishing with punched
    pieces 71, 106
  embossing 60
  layering 59-61, 63-65, 94, 104,
    108, 110, 116
  oversized 56
  paper-piecing embellishments 58,
    102, 121
  repeating 62, 67
  themed 68, 110
  using adhesive foam on 60, 92

F-J

Fonts, graphic 82
Frames, digital photo 25-27, 104-105, 112
Humor 103
Inking 60, 91
Journaling 72-87
  boxes 74, 100, 113, 121
  columns 77
  conversations 80
  curved text 75
  humor in 103
  on photos 25, 34, 76
  unique views 96, 103

O-P

Overlays 32
Paint masking 92
Paper, cut out patterns 10, 15, 19-20, 76, 118
Paper piecing 13, 17, 58, 102, 121
Photos 22-35
  blocks 30, 106, 117
  changing portion to black and white 35
  cropping with a punch 27, 31, 33, 105,
    117-118
  digital mats and frames 25-27, 104-105, 112
  journaling on 25, 34, 76
  overlays 32
  tips 24-25, 29, 95

S-T

Stitching
  by hand 90
  faux 18
Texture, adding to embellishments
  60-61, 64, 69
Themed embellishments 68, 110
Titles 36-53
  die-cut 48, 53
  digital elements 45
  elegant 48
  extra large 43, 113, 119
  layered with shapes 41, 44, 50,
    52, 84, 101
  letter stickers 46
  putting around an object 42
  unique wording 38-39, 103, 112

You and Kate were
We went downtow
and by the time we
full of superheros, v
creatures.

Just a small sampling of our adventures at Mystic Aquarium. I love all the colors and textures within the exhibits. From penguins and sea lions to fish and sting rays, there is so much to see and explore in one afternoon visit.

aquarium
— life

mystic

sisters

Sometimes pictures are just pictures. Something nice to look at and remember a fun time or memory. But sometimes, if you look a bit further a tiny glimpse into the future or maybe a reflection of what has been this photograph from 1944, I see three beautiful girls. Three beautiful very distinct personalities and dispositions. I see these three girls and genes and experiences that have shaped them into the women I know years later. I'm grateful for this picture. Grateful for the chance to see mom and her sisters at an early age. Grateful to discover a little more wonderful women I love.

Every year I am in awe struck at the beautiful colors of the fall season. I never tire of the warm rusts, golds and burgundy. From trees to pumpkins to sunflowers, color explode onto the landscape. Nature is at it's peak in the autumn splendor.

CELEBRATING OVER
THREE SMASH YEARS

SO MUCH HAPPENED BEFORE DOROTHY DROPPED IN

WICKED
A NEW MUSICAL

CHICAGO

TAKE A TOUR OF
DGE   THE THEATRE
7 & 9 TUES THURS SAT

A GLIMPSE OF
Chicago

you have loved all creatures, big and bugs frogs and caterpillars too. April 2008 especially small

UH,
define

computer lab

Three generations of mothers and daughters. Three women who have been given the chance to pass on their knowledge, and experience of what it means to be a woman. Three opportunities to show the love, support and understanding, woman to woman, mother to daughter. Three generations of love.

trick
treat

We joined right in and started to collect the good stuff. By then end, your buckets were full and your legs were tired but a good time was had by all!

Generations
of
LOVE

EVERYDAY, I see this
EVERYDA
EVERYDAY, I listen

And EVERYDAY, I think I couldn't love you more, but then I do.

Want more ideas for Kicking up your projects? Check out these other Memory Makers Books!

Cut Loose

With lots of layouts that illustrate how to break 30 common scrapbooking "rules," *Cut Loose* is bound to spark a bit of rebellion in you and get you creating in fresh new ways.

ISBN-13: 978-1-59963-020-5

ISBN-10: 1599630206

paperback

128 pages

Z1806

Playing with Paper

Lose your fear of patterned paper with ideas for mixing patterns in a wide variety of ways. Includes step-by-step instructions for creative paper techniques.

ISBN-13: 978-1-59963-033-5

ISBN-10: 1-59963-033-8

paperback

128 pages

Z2390

The Scrapbooker's Creativity Kit

Claudine Hellmuth helps jump-start your creativity with word and color cards that are sure to prompt fresh layout ideas. Plus, get inspired by projects illustrating six prompts in action.

ISBN-13: 978-1-59963-031-1

ISBN-10: 1-59963-031-1

paperback

80 pages + 120 cards

Z2280

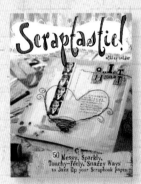

Scraptastic!

Ashley Calder shows you how to experiment with art supplies, try unfamiliar tools, and have fun making messy, sparkly, touchy-feely, snazzy scrapbook pages.

ISBN-13: 978-1-59963-011-3

ISBN-10: 1-59963-011-7

paperback

128 pages

Z1007

These and others Memory Makers titles are available at your local craft retailer, bookstore, online supplier, or visit our Web site at www.mycraftivity.com.

See what's coming up from Memory Makers Books by checking out our blog: www.mycraftivity.com/scrapbooking_papercrafts/blog/